ONE WORLD FOR ONE EARTH

SAVING THE ENVIRONMENT

Philip Sarre was course team chair, *Eleanor Morris* series producer and *Paul Smith* a major contributor to The Open University course and associated TV series *Environment* (U206).

Looking into the Environment study pack

One World for One Earth is also available in the Open University Leisure Series study pack *Looking into the Environment* (PU771), produced in association with the World Wide Fund for Nature. The pack contains a 180-minute video cassette with separate programmes shot on location in the Lake District, Yosemite National Park, Endau Rompin (Malaysia), Niger, Bangkok, Sudbury (Ontario), Denmark, Colorado, Bergen (Norway) and New Delhi. An Activities Booklet explores topics and themes from *One World for One Earth* and the video cassette.

For information about the purchase of complete packs and subsidiary packs (video cassette and Activities Booklet only), please write to: The Learning Materials Sales Office, The Open University, PO Box 188, Milton Keynes MK7 6DH, UK.

First published 1991
Earthscan Publications Ltd
3, Endsleigh Street, London WC1H ODD

Copyright © 1991 The Open University

British Library Cataloguing-in-Publication Data

Sarre, Philip
One World for One Earth: Saving the Environment
I. Title II. Smith, Paul III. Morris, Eleanor
304.2

ISBN 1-85383-119-0

Edited, designed and typeset by The Open University
Production by Bob Towell
Origination by Columbia Offset, Singapore
Manufactured in Italy by Grafedit S.p.A., Bergamo

This book is printed on GARDA Matt Art 115 gsm paper. In common with all GARDA Mill papers, this grade is age-resistant as a result of a special bonding process employed in the papermaking operation, whereby no acid reagents or environmentally harmful chemicals are used.

Earthscan Publications Ltd is an editorially independent subsidiary of the International Institute for Environment and Development (Charity No. 800066).

ONE

WORLD

FOR ONE

EARTH

SAVING THE ENVIRONMENT

PHILIP SARRE & PAUL SMITH

WITH ELEANOR MORRIS

Earthscan Publications Limited, London
in association with
The Open University

Contents

Chapters 1, 2, 4, 6 and 8 were written by Philip Sarre and Chapters 3, 5, 7, 9 and 10 by Paul Smith. Eleanor Morris acted as consultant for the case studies in Chapters 2–9, which were taken from the Open University television series *Environment* (U206).

The authors gratefully acknowledge the help of their colleagues on *Environment*. Special thanks are extended to Mark Edwards/Still Pictures for help with this project.

Introduction

'The Earth is one but the world is not.'
Gro Harlem Brundtland

◀ *Destruction of tropical forests is one of the major environmental problems of the 1990s.*

The environment is humanity's life support system. It supplies us with air, water and food for our bodily survival and with materials and energy for housing, transport and manufactured products. For thousands of years humans have altered environments by hunting, fire and agriculture but most of the change has been gradual, reversible and local. Over the last century or two industrialisation and economic growth have greatly increased the extent and severity of society's impacts on the environment. To loss of species and natural habitats has been added local damage by urbanisation, industrial accidents and waste, regional damage by agricultural chemicals, transnational pollution by acid rain and river pollution, and now global changes to the atmosphere – certainly as regards ozone depletion, possibly leading to global warming. The harmonious integration of natural environmental systems is being damaged by a range of human impacts that seem ill-informed, disorganised and even perverse. Hence the comment from Mrs Brundtland, Prime Minister of Norway, that the Earth is one but the human world is disunited.

After years of media hype, most people are aware of a variety of environmental problems in many parts of the world, but are often confused about how serious they are, why they occur and what should be done about them. These are the questions that this book sets out to answer.

Our approach has a distinctive emphasis: we argue that, in spite of the apparent fragmentation, the whole range of environmental problems, from the survival of the sand lizard and smooth snake on Canford Heath to global atmospheric changes, are logically connected. Indeed, they are connected in two kinds of ways. Firstly, they are connected because 'the Earth is one', in other words because the natural environment has evolved over thousands of millions of years into a complex and finely balanced set of structures and processes. Human impacts are disrupting those natural balances and could destabilise systems in ways for which there is no precedent.

The second set of logical connections are social: we show that the damaging actions of groups like peasants in Niger or Brazil, industrialists in Canada or Thailand and energy suppliers in Denmark or India are crucially influenced by the international system of trade, finance and political power. So, whereas many writers on environmental issues stress the *differences* between so-called First, Second and Third worlds, we stress the *connections* between them. Focusing on the connections should not be allowed to obscure the differences, but we believe that referring to connections between more and less developed countries avoids the impression of three separate worlds and also allows the recognition of differences within 'worlds', such as the differences between the relative prosperity of some oil exporting and newly industrialising countries and the abject poverty of the least developed countries.

Our title, and our argument, does more than recognise that there are vital connections between differently developed parts of the world. It points to the negative consequences of the existing connections and argues that they are in no one's best interests. To overcome the degradation of environments (and of poor people) world-wide we urgently need to respond in a more unified way. Initially this means closer collaboration between governments but ultimately it requires greater equity between countries and people. Only then can we achieve one world in a sense which implies the high degree of integration which already exists for the one Earth.

The two kinds of interconnectedness in environmental relationships (the natural and the social) determine the structure of this book. First, in Chapter l, we outline the main features of the natural life support systems on which we depend, showing that they have evolved over time and involve close relationships between living things and inanimate processes. Then subsequent chapters address selected aspects of human impacts on the environment, showing why they occur, how they change natural systems and how society is responding. Finally, the last two chapters draw together these social responses into proposals which combine individual, corporate, governmental and international changes. To prevent the discussion becoming excessively abstract and general, the eight central chapters each include a detailed case study and show how the particular events in the case relate to broader questions.

Many of the issues that the book discusses are extremely complex, so we have had to select and simplify to present the main features and principles. The main text carries the basic argument and is illustrated with photographs worth many thousands of words in showing what situations look and feel like. From time to time we include boxes, tables and more complex illustrations so that you can pursue points in greater depth if you want to. But our main aim is to establish a general framework to which you can relate more detailed treatments in the media and other books. The framework includes a knowledge of natural and social processes, an understanding of why they occur and a consciousness of the values, implicit or explicit, which underlie people's actions in relation to environment, including the values which underlie our call for 'one world'.

CHAPTER 1

Earth without humanity

Over the last two decades, scientific debate about life on other planets has recognised that something we usually take for granted is in fact remarkable. This is that conditions on Earth are 'just right' for living things. This is all the more surprising when we compare the Earth with Mars and Venus. All three planets are formed from the same materials and started with atmospheres consisting largely of carbon dioxide. Today Mars has virtually no atmosphere, so temperatures on the surface fluctuate enormously between day and night and average – 60 °C. Venus, on the contrary, has a very dense atmosphere of carbon dioxide and surface temperatures average 460 °C. By contrast, large areas of the Earth's surface have fairly equable temperature regimes as well as moderate variations in wind and water availability. Just as Goldilocks found some things in the three bears' cottage too hot or too cold, too hard or too soft, but others 'just right', so the Earth is remarkably well suited to complex life forms. The key to these conditions is the nature of the Earth's atmosphere, because without it surface temperatures would, like the moon, average –18 °C.

When we look at the Earth's atmosphere and ask how it happens to be 'just right' for life, we find that the mystery deepens. Geologists have been able to show that the present atmosphere is completely different from the atmosphere which existed in the early part of the Earth's history.

Geologists now believe that the Earth formed by the accretion of particles of matter about 4,600 million years ago. Gravitational attraction progressively forced these particles together and raised their temperature until they solidified and even melted, generating volcanic processes. Massive quantities of carbon dioxide and water were emitted by volcanoes. They were held by the Earth's gravity to form its first atmosphere and ocean. Then, as now, carbon dioxide allowed solar radiation to pass through to the surface but absorbed radiation from the surface and slowed its escape to space, so atmospheric temperatures climbed to about 28 °C. But an atmosphere of carbon dioxide would be inhospitable to all known plants and animals. How has it been transformed into its present state, with 79 per cent nitrogen, 21 per cent oxygen and small traces of carbon dioxide, water vapour and rare gases?

▲ *Cloud patterns both indicate atmospheric circulation and intercept incoming solar radiation.*

The changes to the atmosphere can be reconstructed by geologists because the rock deposits of a particular period relate to the chemical content of the atmosphere. About 3,500 million years ago, extensive layers of 'banded ironstones' were laid down, containing iron compounds which could only exist in an oxygen-free atmosphere. One thousand million years later, mats of blue-green algae had appeared and were carrying out one of

◄ *Previous page*
Familiar to millions as the gateway to Britain, the White Cliffs of Dover have a deeper environmental significance as storehouses of earlier atmospheric carbon dioxide.

the crucial processes of life – photosynthesis. In photosynthesis, the energy from the sun is used by green plants to combine carbon dioxide and water into sugars, and oxygen is given off. Once the blue-green algae had liberated some oxygen into the air, microscopic marine plants (called phytoplankton) came into existence, strengthening fixation of carbon through photosynthesis. Some of these plants, and hence this carbon, were locked away in sediments in the deep ocean. By 2,000 million years ago there was enough oxygen in the atmosphere to prevent the formation of banded ironstones: iron-rich rocks were now 'red beds', coloured by iron compounds similar to those in rust.

During the ensuing 1,000 million years a new form of carbon fixation was added: some animals and plants began forming limestone skeletons or shells. Under the right conditions, these were deposited in shallow seas as chalk or limestone. In the process, the oxygen content of the atmosphere increased progressively until land plants and animals could become established. About 300 million years ago there was a major period of coal formation: this was another way in which carbon in plant remains was made unavailable to the oxygen in the atmosphere. Very recently (in geological terms) humans have discovered that, just as plants and animals combine carbon compounds with oxygen in the process of respiration and so generate energy, so coal can be burned in air to give off heat, releasing carbon dioxide. Before this technical breakthrough, the balance between photosynthesis and respiration had removed almost all carbon from the atmosphere and increased oxygen content to its practical limit. If oxygen was any more plentiful, there would be a more serious danger of plant remains bursting into flame spontaneously. However, the combination of oxygen with ammonia released from volcanoes produced nitrogen and water, and the stable nature of nitrogen moderates the reactivity of air.

To sum up: over thousands of millions of years blue-green algae and plants have removed carbon from the atmosphere. The presence of deep oceans, shallow seas and swamps has provided a variety of ways for this carbon to be locked away from oxygen. In the process, the atmosphere has become cooler as the proportion of carbon dioxide decreased, and large quantities of oxygen have been released into the atmosphere where it is available for respiration and combustion. The 'just right' conditions for complex life forms have actually been created by simpler forms of life. As living things have evolved into more complex forms, the environment has evolved in parallel and the actual adjustment of living things and inanimate materials and processes is more than coincidental.

But the balance between atmosphere and life is not static. Change one and the other must respond. So the dramatic changes in animal and plant life brought about by population and economic growth are bound to change the atmosphere, and hence other related systems. Several of these systems are crucial to natural vegetation and agriculture, so the next step is to sketch the carbon and water cycles and to recognise the vital role of solar radiation as the driving energy source of all these natural systems.

The carbon cycle

As described above, past processes have taken huge quantities of carbon from the atmosphere and locked it into geological reservoirs. The estimated amounts are shown in Figure 1.1. In fact 'locked' is too strong a word as there are major flows between reservoirs. Most of these are natural, but in recent decades society has added to them.

The natural processes would be in balance in the short term. Carbon dioxide is taken from the atmosphere by photosynthesis and by dissolution in the oceans. Carbon dioxide is released into the atmosphere by the respiration of organisms on land and, via sea water, in the oceans. Some plant and animal remains are locked into peat bogs or ocean sediments and so not returned to the atmosphere. Limestone and corals are still forming, locking calcium carbonate away – but carbon dioxide is still being released from rocks through volcanic activity. The size of the different reservoirs and the rate of flow between them are very different and the amount of carbon dioxide in the atmosphere is minute compared with the amounts to be found elsewhere.

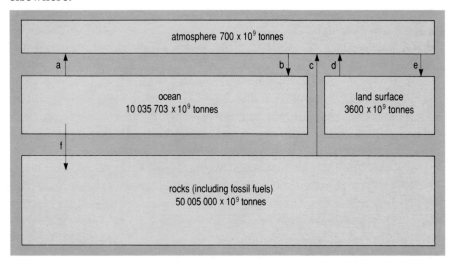

Figure 1.1 *The carbon cycle, showing major reservoirs and flows with quantities in thousand million tonnes. Not all the flows can be measured, but of those which can (e) is the largest at 70 x 10^9 tonnes per year. Only part of (b) is known: marine organisms absorb about 45 x 10^9 tonnes per year, but the ocean itself may dissolve much more than this.*

A newly significant input of carbon dioxide to the atmosphere is that released by the combustion of fossil fuels. At 5,000 million (i.e. 5×10^9) tonnes per year, this is small compared to the natural flows, but it is 0.7 per cent of the amount in the atmosphere, so it could increase atmospheric concentration substantially in a few decades if the other flows fail to adjust. Observations over the last few decades suggest that about half of this extra carbon dioxide is absorbed in ways not yet identified, but that the concentration in the atmosphere has risen from 315 parts per million (p.p.m.) in 1957 to 350 p.p.m. in 1987. In comparison to this, air trapped in ice sheets over the last 160,000 years has varied between 180 and 300 p.p.m. So the current level is higher than in recent geological history, and on current trends it could be 600 p.p.m. by the end of the next century. The effects of this will be discussed in Chapter 8.

The water cycle

Everyone knows that rain falls from the clouds and that some reaches rivers which flow to the sea. Anyone living in Britain can see that the clouds bring most rain when they come in from the Atlantic. A moment's reflection suggests that the clouds obtain their moisture from evaporation from the sea. There is in fact a cycle in which water moves from the sea to the air, on to land and back to the sea. Scientists have made estimates of the amounts of water present on land, in the sea and in the air and of the annual rates of flow between them. These are shown in Figure 1.2.

A crucial feature of this cycle is that most water is in the oceans and very little in the atmosphere. Comparing the rates of flow into and out of the atmosphere with the average amount present, it appears that a particular droplet of water only remains in the atmosphere a week or two before falling as rain or snow. Conversely, a drop of water falling into the sea remains, on average, for 4,000 years. This makes the atmosphere very variable and sensitive to inputs and outputs.

Of course, the figures given are averaged over the whole globe over a year and this conceals great differences between areas and over time. The tropics and hilly areas exposed to mid-latitude westerly winds may receive several hundred centimetres of rain a year while deserts and polar areas may receive only 10 or 20 centimetres of rain or its equivalent in snow. The availability of rain seriously affects plant growth, but plants also have the effect of increasing amounts of water entering the atmosphere. As well as evaporating from the surface, some water is taken up by plants and transpired through leaf pores into the air. The total amount of water returning to the air as water vapour, a process called evapotranspiration, may be much greater than the amount evaporated. In turn, greater humidity encourages more rain and more plant growth, so yet again natural systems show complex self-organisations.

But it's not enough just to admire the elegance of natural cycles. We also need to ask 'what makes them go?'.

◀ *The water cycle concentrates solar energy in a way which allows non-polluting and sustainable power generation.*

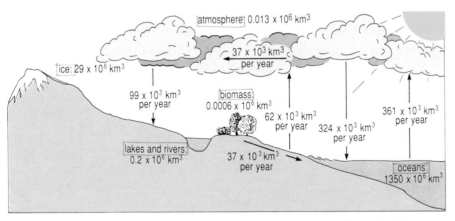

Figure 1.2 *The water cycle. Quantities in each reservoir are given in million cubic kilometres (10^6 km^3) and flows, indicated by arrows, in thousand cubic kilometres (10^3 km^3).*

Powering the cycles

Like a pedal cycle, natural cycles such as those of water and carbon require an outside source of energy. It's no great surprise that their source of energy is the Sun, but this in fact identifies a basic principle: the energy in environmental processes *flows* continuously, arriving from and being lost to space, while matter is present in constant amounts and can only be transformed between different states. The flows of energy are exceedingly complex and include the temporary storage of solar energy in the form of fossil fuels, but only a small fraction of the energy that reaches the Earth is stored in this way. What happens to the rest?

The broad pattern of energy throughput is shown in Figure 1.3. Almost one-third of the solar energy which reaches the atmosphere is reflected back into space by dust and clouds. About one-fifth is absorbed by the atmosphere before reaching the surface; just under half reaches the land or sea surface, of which a quarter is reflected straight back to space, half powers the evaporation of water vapour from land and sea and the remainder is reradiated and absorbed by the atmosphere, warming it and causing vertical circulation; somewhat less than one per cent drives the wind and currents and a mere 0.2 per cent is used in photosynthesis. The enormous quantity of solar energy in the atmosphere is demonstrated by the fact that

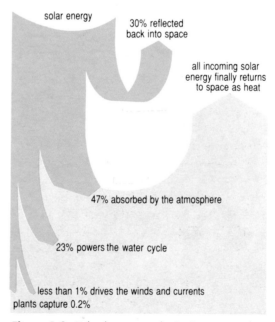

Figure 1.3 *What happens to the Sun's energy in the atmosphere?*

even the tiny proportion used in photosynthesis is 30 or so times as much as the amount of energy used by human society.

Of course, in practice the amounts of solar radiation reaching the surface of the Earth vary greatly, depending on the angle of incidence and on cloud and dust cover. Because the Earth's axis is inclined towards the Sun, the apparent direction of the Sun varies from $23^1/_2$ °N in July to $23^1/_2$ °S in January and polar areas receive a substantial amount of radiation in summer. This is one way that temperature is raised at the poles. Another way is that atmospheric and ocean circulation combine to transfer heat from equatorial regions towards the poles. This transfer is associated with distinctive pressure, wind and precipitation regimes in particular areas.

A world without Homo sapiens

Before we move on to analyse human impacts on natural environments, it will be useful to consider what the world would be like without human intervention. This relies in part on present and past observations of undisturbed areas, in part on analyses of natural records like pollen trapped in peat bogs, and in part on ecological understanding of the way climate, soils, plants and animals influence each other.

The central concept is that the climatic patterns mentioned above would (if there were no intervention from society) produce distinctive patterns of soil, animals and plants called biomes. If the continents were rectangular and of even height, there would be a series of parallel bands. At the equator, tropical rain forest is the vegetation suited to the climate. Then, moving away from the equator, a wide intermediate zone of savanna (grassland with scattered trees) leads into the hot deserts of 20–30 °N and S. Another transition zone alternating wet and dry seasons is familiar as the Mediterranean climate. Then mid-latitude deciduous woodland grades into coniferous woodland. As temperatures fall too low for tree growth, there is a band of tundra, with low plants and lichens in summer and continuous snow cover in winter. Finally there are the polar ice caps.

In practice, the irregular shape of the continents, their varying height above sea level and the effects of seasonal heating and cooling in the continental interiors produces a much more fragmented pattern of natural vegetation (see Figure 1.4). In particular, this shows that there are strong contrasts between the west and east coasts of most continents. The sheer size of Asia helps to break up climatic and vegetational patterns, with both desert and tundra conditions widespread at the same latitude as Spain.

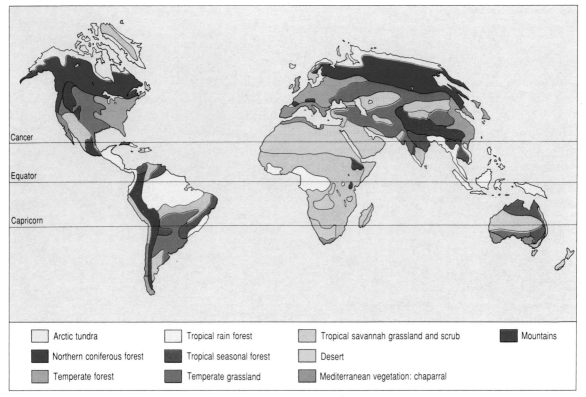

Cancer

Equator

Capricorn

☐ Arctic tundra	☐ Tropical rain forest	☐ Tropical savannah grassland and scrub	■ Mountains
■ Northern coniferous forest	■ Tropical seasonal forest	☐ Desert	
☐ Temperate forest	■ Temperate grassland	■ Mediterranean vegetation: chaparral	

Figure 1.4 *Distribution of the major types of world vegetation.*

In spite of the fragmented pattern and resulting variety within biomes, it is still the case that in the long-term, climate, soils, vegetation and animal life in broad areas adjust to each other to form recognisable communities. These have been studied in detail at a local scale and show how living things and their environments form complex organisations called ecosystems.

Ecosystems

An ecosystem is an organised community of plants and animals in a particular kind of environment. Like the Earth as a whole, an ecosystem is powered by a throughput of solar energy and cycles of nutrients between its components. A small amount of the solar energy reaching the surface is used in the leaves of green plants to synthesise sugars as a source of chemical energy. Part (up to one-tenth) of this energy is acquired by grazing animals (herbivores) and used to power their activities. In turn, a part of the herbivores' energy may be acquired by carnivores. As plants and animals die, they become dead organic matter. Most of this is used as a source of energy and nutrients by decomposers (including animals, fungi and bacteria) and broken down into simpler forms which become available as plant nutrients. Some survives for longer periods as wood or peat. The flow of energy is illustrated in Figure 1.5.

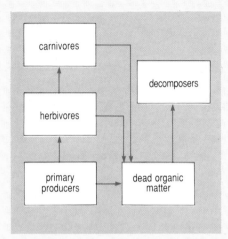

Figure 1.5
Compartments of a diagrammatic ecosystem, showing the direction of energy flows.

However, this energy flow can only occur if plants are also provided with nutrients and water. The main nutrients, as every gardener knows, are nitrogen, phosphates and potash, but sulphur and other minerals are needed in smaller quantities. The ultimate source of nitrogen is the air and that of all other minerals is the breakdown of rock, but they only become available to plants in the very special mixture of fine particles and organic remains which we call soil. So the soil is an important link in the crucial mineral cycles and an impoverished soil can restrict plant development in other-wise favourable circumstances.

A particularly important mineral cycle is that of nitrogen, both because it is an essential building block of proteins and because its availability is the major limitation on growth in many ecosystems. Atmospheric nitrogen is unavailable to plants, so before use it must be 'fixed', or converted into ammonia, which in nature is done mainly by soil bacteria, especially *Rhizobium* living in nodules on the roots of legumes. Ammonia may be assimilated by plants, converted to nitrite or lost back to the air. Nitrite may be converted to nitrate, the main nitrogenous plant food, or to nitrogen gas which can also be lost back to the air (denitrification). Nitrates are soluble in water and can be leached (washed) out of the soil in wet periods. Organic compounds including nitrogen may also reach the soil in the form of dead organic matter. Some amino acids can be taken up directly by plants, but most are decomposed to the simple mineral forms – ammonia and nitrate – which are available for uptake by plants or are lost by leaching or denitrification.

The variety of living things which coexist in ecosystems and biomes is staggering. At present 1.8 million species are known to science and estimates of the numbers of species not yet described range from 2–25 million. The estimates are uncertain: some biomes have been researched in detail, but others are more complex and less researched.

The British Isles have been researched as intensively as anywhere. About 1,600 species of plants are known and this is probably close to the real figure. Animals are much more numerous, especially insects of which 23,500 have been described, probably about 90 per cent of the true total. In Britain, as elsewhere, among recorded species animals are more numerous than plants. The majority of animals are insects and the majority of insects are beetles. Why evolution should have produced so many species of beetle is not known.

▼ Temperate woodlands contain far fewer species and are much more intensively researched than tropical forests.

The opposite extreme among biomes is the tropical forest. Whereas Britain contains about 70 species of tree, samples of Amazon rain forest have been found to contain up to 283 species of tree *per hectare*, to say nothing of ground flora, climbers and epiphytes. Moreover, a nearby hectare would not contain the same collection of trees but a largely different set. By comparing many relatively small samples in different tropical forests, scientists have estimated that there are about 50,000 species of tree. Compared to numbers of insects, this is a modest total: one entomologist used insecticides to investigate numbers of insects and found up to 1,100 species of beetle living on a single tree, of which 160 appeared to be specific to that variety of tree. At that rate, there would be 8 million species of beetle in the world's tropical forests, and this is the kind of thinking that produces the higher estimates of total numbers of species. Indeed, one study in Indonesia found twice as many species in the soil – chiefly decomposers called springtails – as there were insects in the canopy.

Tropical forests cover only one-fifteenth of the Earth's land surface but probably contain over half its species. This is as true of the higher animals as of trees and beetles. In fact only four countries – Brazil, Madagascar, Zaire and Indonesia – contain three-quarters of these animals. The enormous variety of the tropical forests seems to result from the very long time that this biome has been established. By contrast, temperate coniferous and deciduous forests have had to recolonise areas since the last glaciation and so have only had about 10,000 years to develop their variety.

The rain forests are the home of most primate species, but even the remote areas are threatened, as are these mountain gorillas.

Perhaps the only species which is less numerous in tropical forests than in other biomes is *Homo sapiens*. This is because it is much more difficult to convert tropical forest land to agricultural use than is true of temperate, including Mediterranean, woodland or savana or prairie grassland. These problems of conversion will be discussed in Chapter 3.

For now it only remains to sum up the picture of what the world (would have) looked like before *Homo sapiens* began to develop culturally and technologically. The vast variety and precise organisation of natural systems have led many past commentators to speculate on how such events could have occurred without a designer. One recent debate likened the organising principle to the work of a 'blind watchmaker'. But we would want to emphasise that the natural world is much more complex and impressive than a watch or indeed *any* known mechanism. The fact that living things, atmosphere and soils have evolved together over many millennia has led not just to complex mutual adjustment in the short term. It has built up dependencies and feedback relationships which are self-balancing. Each element of the whole is 'just right' in its particular niche. Just as the three bears reacted to Goldilocks' intrusion by chasing her out of their home, ecosystems react to disturbance as if trying to preserve the

▽ *The era of glasnost revealed massive pollution problems in the Soviet bloc as a result of reliance on outdated technology.*

previous balance. However, if the disturbances become too extreme a whole ecosystem may become unviable and change rapidly towards a new balance. In nature, that new balance will almost always be simpler, less efficient and less resilient than the original ecosystem. Human society has increasingly set out to replace natural ecosystems with agricultural systems which will produce more of what humans demand. It always takes a great effort to install and maintain new systems and there are often unanticipated problems. This is still more so as industrial activities grow in extent and complexity, and have greater impacts on natural systems.

In recent years many environmentalists, following James Lovelock, have become interested in the Gaia hypothesis. This develops the idea of a highly organised global system of living things and natural processes almost to the degree of possessing will. Gaia was the Greek goddess of the Earth. From this viewpoint any disruptive influence will be counteracted and eliminated by Gaia and the obvious candidate for elimination is human society. This may seem a rather cynical view to many people, but in our view it is in some ways optimistic because it suggests that the planet can eliminate human society and revert to a golden age of natural systems in harmony. It is more probable that human society will continue to disrupt natural systems and grow in numbers and activity. In such a world individuals will be left with reduced access to degraded natural systems and possibly with falling quality of life and life expectancy. Rather than face either future, we should use our undoubted ingenuity to change society and coexist more harmoniously with natural systems.

CHAPTER 2

Valued environments: environmental values

'A conservationist is a man who concerns himself
with the beauties of nature in roughly inverse
proportion to the number of people who can enjoy
them.'

J.K. Galbraith, 1958.

Chapter 1 has discussed how the world would work without the human species. But most of what we see in the world has been influenced by past or present human activities. Only in the heart of the desert or the tropical forest, on the high mountains, the remote islands and in the wilderness park does the environment appear natural. This chapter shows how the present situation came about. An important part of this story is the growth in the extent and severity of human impacts on natural environments. Many people are surprised to find that hunter-gatherer societies were already modifying their environments tens of thousands of years ago, though they are less surprised to learn of the growing impacts of agricultural and industrial society. An account of how human impacts grew gives some clues to the causes of current problems. Even more vital is a knowledge of the development of environmentalist ideas, not just as an academic study of past ideas but as a contribution to developing our own responses to the unprecedented threats which we now face. So the chapter starts by considering the ideas of some early environmentalists, goes on to illustrate the growing human impacts on environments and ends by explaining how environmentalist ideas made a quantum leap in the late 1960s.

Pioneer environmentalists

Many simple societies had customs which sustained the environmental systems they depended on. Some conscious discussions of environmental management can be found in the literature of early civilisations. This will be briefly discussed below. But the pioneers who are most relevant to today's environmentalists emerged in the nineteenth century. We will look at key figures in England and America whose influence is still alive today. In particular we will focus on people and organisations whose ideas were stimulated and shaped by their attachment to two highly valued areas.

The English Lake District and California's Yosemite National Park are among the premier national parks of today, with 14 and 4 million visitors a year respectively. Their histories have some similarities and some curious differences. The Lake District has been progressively settled over several thousand years, but was not designated as a park until 1951. Yosemite Valley was only discovered by white people in 1857, but was the first wild area in the world to be set aside when it became a State Park in 1864. So the early British environmentalists had less help from government than was the case in the USA. However, both groups had to change public attitudes to preserve the areas they loved.

◁ *Previous page*
For millennia, human societies have dramatically altered their environments even in remote and inhospitable areas.

The clear waters of the Merced River and the distinctive shape of Half Dome emphasise why Yosemite was the world's first scenic reserve.

In the eighteenth century the main attitude to wild land in both countries was that it should be tamed and exploited. The early settlers in the USA had to clear forests and build all the facilities they needed for survival, which often extended to the clearance of the native people who had preceded them. In the UK even seasoned travellers like Daniel Defoe abhorred and avoided the uplands. Where the resources were available, artificial landscapes were constructed, with planned vistas and viewing points. Indeed the earliest visitors to the Lake District carried guide books to lead them to selected viewing points and even Claude glasses (tinted convex mirrors) through which the landscape would look more like a painting.

The artificiality of this way of experiencing landscape was challenged by the Romantic poets, especially William Wordsworth, who was born and educated in the Lake District and, after a period at Cambridge and travelling in France, returned to live at Dove Cottage, Grasmere, in 1799. In his poetry, he celebrated two aspects of the Lake District – the beauties of the landscape and the sterling qualities of the inhabitants. The crux of his position lay in direct personal experience of a landscape imbued with spiritual presences and an appreciation of the harmony between farmers, shepherds, their buildings and fields and the natural landscape as they struggled to make a living. Wordsworth was offended, even appalled, by the new buildings being commissioned by wealthy incomers, by the planting of alien trees and, later in his life, by the proposed extension of the railway to Windermere. He wrote his *Guide to the Lakes*, first published in 1810 and revised in many subsequent editions, to persuade visitors and new residents to adopt appropriate values and to adjust their behaviour and new developments so that they would not destroy the character of the area they sought out. His position had many weaknesses – he had only a limited scientific knowledge of how the Lake District environment worked and his political attitudes became rather elitist – but his insistence on direct personal engagement with the landscape helped transform the way people experienced their environments.

Patterdale, the Lake District.

'These Tourists, Heaven preserve us! needs must live
A profitable life: some glance along,
Rapid and gay, as if the earth were air,
And they were butterflies to wheel about
Long as the summer lasted: some, as wise,
Perched on the forehead of a jutting crag,
Pencil in hand and book upon the knee,
Will look and scribble, scribble on and look,
Until a man might travel twelve stout miles,
Or reap an acre of his neighbour's corn...'

William Wordsworth, 'The Brothers', Lyrical Ballads, Volume Two, 1800.

In 1831 Wordsworth was visited by a New Englander, Ralph Waldo Emerson, who was to have a similar effect on the way Americans experienced nature. His essays, poetry and lectures argued that there was a mystical relationship between people, nature and what he called the Oversoul. He emphasised the positive contribution of wilderness to American life and indeed this was taken up by many Americans in the nineteenth century as a test of character in the expansion of the frontier, and in the twentieth century in widespread support for the preservation of areas where individuals could still find a 'wilderness experience'. Today's American environmentalists are more conscious of one of Emerson's disciples, Henry David Thoreau, who in 1845 left Concord to build and live in a cabin near Walden Pond. His diaries and the book *Walden* are classics in environmentalist literature. In spite of his theoretical espousal of wilderness, Emerson only visited the West late in his life, but when he did one of his priorities was to visit Yosemite and meet the man who did more to promote wilderness preservation than anyone else – John Muir.

John Muir was born in Scotland in 1838 and brought up on a farm in Wisconsin. In 1868, after an accident that nearly cost him his sight, he travelled to Yosemite in search of 'somewhere wild'. In fact the valley was already quite developed, with hotels, farms growing crops to feed visitors and horses, and a number of paved trails up the valley side. Muir used the valley as a base for long hikes into the high Sierras, where one of his early contributions was to recognise long before the academic geologists that the dramatic landscapes had been caused by glaciers. As well as solitary walking, he began to lead other walkers, became a celebrated raconteur and writer, and so communicated his experiences and sense of wonder to a wide public. He was vital to the campaign to have the 1,200 square miles of high country designated as a national park in 1890. In 1892 he was asked to become president of a new club set up initially by academics from Berkeley – The Sierra Club. In 1903 he led President Roosevelt on a camping trip in Yosemite and persuaded him into a massive expansion of national parks, forests and monuments over the next few years. But though his successes were great, his career ended with a failure: in spite of vigorous campaigning, the preservationists were unable to persuade Congress to refuse San Francisco permission to dam Hetch Hetchy – the second major valley in Yosemite Park. The city's arguments were supported by Gifford Pinchot, the United States Chief Forester and advocate of conservation interpreted as 'wise use'. Even the Sierra Club was divided by the issue and in the atmosphere of sympathy for San Francisco after the 1906 earthquake, permission was given and the dam built. John Muir died, some say of a broken heart, in 1914.

'Unfortunately man is in the woods and waste and pure
destruction are making rapid headway. If the importance
of forests are at all understood even from an economic
standpoint, their preservation would call forth the
watchful attention of the government.

'Thousands of tired, nerve shaken, over-civilised people
are beginning to find out that going to the mountains is
going home, that wildness is a necessity and mountains,
parks and reservations are useful not only as fountains of
timber and irrigating rivers but as fountains of life.'

John Muir

A contemporary of Muir's, and Wordsworth's successor as an advocate
of Lake District preservation, was a man very different from both of them.
John Ruskin had had an early ambition to be a geologist but, like Wordsworth
before him, he found it difficult to adjust his essentially biblical view of
nature to accommodate the new scientific ideas about geology and evolution.
Although it had been proved in 1840 that the Lake District exhibited all the
signs of erosion by glaciers, Ruskin was never able to accept the idea.
Instead of geology, he turned to the history of art and architecture and soon
became a celebrity, especially as he championed the radical new style of
Turner. However, Ruskin reacted strongly to the growing despoliation of
Britain by industry and developed a radical critique of industrial society.
He was the first to recognise that environmental damage, urban squalor
and social injustice were products of industrialisation. He proposed many
changes, including town planning and a welfare state, and inspired more
practical people to develop new institutions which would change society
towards the more humane and environmentally benign state that he
envisaged. Even after he resigned his post as Professor of Art at Oxford (in
protest at having to lecture next to a vivisection laboratory) and went to live
at Brantwood on the shores of Coniston Water in 1871, he was conscious of
mining activity and of air pollution from the booming iron works and
shipyards of Barrow-in-Furness and Workington. He conceived the idea of
a 'plague wind' spreading over Europe and lapsed into severe depression in
his last years.

Just as in California, the Lake District preservationists were stung
into more effective action by a proposal to build a reservoir. In 1875 the city
of Manchester – then the biggest and fastest growing industrial city in the
world – sought to build a reservoir at Thirlmere in the heart of the Lake
District. The Thirlmere Defence Association was formed by Robert Somervell,
a local industrialist, with Canon Rawnsley (a former student of Ruskin's)

as spokesman. They succeeded in defeating Manchester's private Parliamentary Bill in 1878 – the first time that environmentalist objections were allowed to be heard in such a case – but in 1879 Manchester's urgent need for pure water for domestic supply and the cotton industry prevailed and Thirlmere became a reservoir. The response of the preservationists was to form the Lake District Defence Society as a permanent body so that they could campaign for preservation and respond immediately to new threats. Interestingly, only a small minority of the membership lived in the Lake District. Most came from London or the large industrial cities. Many were clergymen, academics and teachers, some from colleges in the USA. After Thirlmere, they were successful in warding off any further major developments.

The Lake District also played a leading part in stimulating the formation of the National Trust in 1894. Canon Rawnsley joined with Octavia Hill (who had been inspired by Ruskin to set up housing charities) and Robert Hunter (of the Commons Preservation Society) to incorporate the National Trust as a charity to hold valued landscapes permanently. This organisation has been so successful that, in addition to property all over the country, it now owns a quarter of the Lake District.

The contrast between the National Trust and the Sierra Club is a fascinating indicator of national style. The National Trust was formed in the home of the Duke of Westminster and continues to have close relations with the landowning class. Since its foundation its emphasis has moved away from preservation of landscape to the preservation of historic houses. Having chosen to concentrate on preservation through ownership, it faces the problem of combining economically viable use of its land with preservation of its character. The Sierra Club was more middle class in its origins and focused on creating a constituency in favour of wilderness preservation rather than on direct ownership. In doing so, it relied on the early commitment of the US government to conservation and on the availability of national park designation and the National Park Service as a form of management.

Acceptance of the idea of national park designation came much later in Britain. Only after World War II, during the period of enthusiasm for creation of a comprehensive welfare state under the Attlee Government, was the National Parks and Access to the Countryside Act passed. When they were designated in the 1950s, the British parks had major differences from those in the USA, South Africa and Canada: they had a substantial resident population (45,000 in the Lake District) and the park authorities had to act through planning powers rather than owning and enjoying absolute power as in Yosemite. So, as well as preserving the valued landscape and improving visitor access, the British park managers had to

The building of the Keswick bypass through the Lake District National Park demonstrates the tension between conservation and increased access.

take account of the needs of the local population and economy. This has led to compromise and even muddle. In 1989 the UK government's application to have the Lake District recognised as a World Heritage Site was not approved by UNESCO, partly on the grounds that sites are classified as natural *or* cultural and the Lake District had claimed to be both, and partly on the grounds that the powers of the park authority were not strong enough to give it adequate protection. So as a tool of preservation, the UK national parks have been found wanting. But a more positive reaction exists: that their experience of pursuing both environmental quality and economic prosperity is a proving ground for a form of environmentalism which goes beyond trying to preserve a few remnants of a natural past towards one which injects environmental values into all decisions.

This is a position advocated by one of America's leading environ-mentalists. David Brower grew up in California and rose to be the first executive director of the Sierra Club. In tne 1960s he was forced out of his position because the elder statesmen of the Club found him too aggressive in his public and legislative campaigning. They feared that he was alien-ating government support and prejudicing their finances by publication of lavish books, photographs and films. Brower's response was to found a new organisation which was not restricted by its heritage to defence of particular valued environments: Friends of the Earth was set up in 1970 as an international, mass membership, campaigning body which could promote environmentalist responses to the whole range of twentieth century threats. But how had these threats come about?

The growth of human impacts on environments

The extent and severity of human impacts on environments depend on the way societies organise production. Three broad methods have existed. For most of human history, human groups were small and mobile and lived as hunter-gatherers. From about 10,000 BC, agricultural societies began to appear, at first in the Near East and then spreading into Asia and Europe. Over the last few centuries, industrialised societies have appeared, starting in the UK and spreading into Europe, the USA and East Asia. Industrialisation has not only transformed relations with the environment in industrial areas or countries, it has done so even in surviving agricultural and hunting societies. This 'rippling out' of the effects of industrialisation was felt by Ruskin and Muir a century ago; now it covers the whole globe and even reaches into space. So where early impacts on environments were local and often reversible, today's impacts are global and perhaps irreversible.

However, we should not underestimate the effects of past societies. Hunting and gathering could only support very sparse populations but they were practised for tens of thousands of years in environments from tropical forests to the high Arctic, and some remnants exist even today in remote and extreme locations. Many such groups may have existed in balance with their environments for long periods, taking only a proportion of the yield of fruits, vegetables and animals. But there is ample evidence that some groups had significant impacts. The first major impact, evident in the fossil record, is the extinction of large animals by human groups. Such extinctions were numerous in North America but can also be traced in Australia, New Zealand, Madagascar and Indonesia. Large animals, mainly mammals but also flightless birds and marsupials, often had few natural enemies and long life spans, and consequently low rates of reproduction. As such, they would have been quickly reduced in numbers by hunters. The loss of major species was itself a significant change, but it would also have led to change in vegetation cover because of reduced grazing pressure. Other groups have changed vegetation cover directly and deliberately by the use of fire: this was done to favour certain species over others and even to ensure that seeds or nuts were all produced at a given time. Fire was extensively used by Australian aborigines and was a crucial factor in moulding the distinctive vegetation cover which European migrants thought of as natural. Regular burning has also been used in the Mediterranean lands, at first by hunters and later by shepherds, to produce the distinctive thorny scrub called *maquis* or *garrigue* in preference to the natural cover of oak. There are some indications of hunter-gatherers using other techniques, such as diversion of stream channels, but change to vegetation cover by fire and modification of animal numbers are the most extensive effects. Surviving hunter-gatherer societies show complex adaptations to ensure long-term survival, both in terms of detailed knowledge of potential food resources and in terms of beliefs and customs which prevent them from damaging the systems they depend on. Known cases of negative effects, such as the over-hunting of beaver in nineteenth century Canada or elephant poaching in contemporary East Africa, result from international markets which provide the demand the hunters respond to.

Settled agriculture, starting in about 9,000 BC, and pastoralism, which emerged somewhat later, have involved much more systematic environmental change than hunting. Perhaps the greatest single change was deforestation: the temperate woodlands of Europe, North America, the Mediterranean lands and China were all decimated by agriculturalists. Nowhere was this process more dramatic than in the UK where a largely forest covered island was transformed into the least forested part of Europe. In turn, deforestation exposed the soil to erosion and much soil was lost, especially in drier and hillier areas. The loss of the cedar forests of Lebanon and the erosion of hillsides in Greece were already being commented upon 2,000 years ago. In long-settled areas some riddles persist: the Romans

◁ *Two thousand years ago, Greek authors were already commenting on soil erosion brought about by deforestation.*

grew wheat in areas of North Africa which are now desert – but is it the climate that has changed or is it a result of mismanagement? A very early environmental change was brought about by irrigation – indeed it was crucial to some of the earliest civilisations. But where some of those civilisations collapsed, as they did in Mesopotamia, it is difficult to establish whether the breakdown was brought about by environmental change, the collapse of the necessary social organisation or some combination of the two. But irrigation has transformed areas as diverse as Egypt and the mountains and plains of South and East Asia, where tier after tier of terraces are a testament to generations of sustained effort by agriculturalists.

Agriculturalists have also transformed landscapes by drainage, from simple field ditches to the massive dykes and channels used, especially by the Dutch, to reclaim land from the sea. The use of windmills to pump away surplus water is a reminder that early agriculturalists could call not only on the energy of domesticated draft animals but on sources of energy like wind and water.

Wind power was also crucial to the sailing ships that drew the world together in the fifteenth and sixteenth centuries. Trade in precious metals, agricultural products and handicrafts contributed to larger-scale production of luxury goods from gold to spices and silk. Crop plants were spread

▶ *The Dutch have transformed their country by reclaiming land from the sea.*

to new areas, most famously in the establishment of Brazilian rubber trees in Malaya. Natural vegetation was increasingly replaced by plantations of tea, coffee, cocoa, rubber and sugar. In turn, the profits from trade created the institutions and markets which could finance and sell new industrial products.

It was no coincidence that Britain, the country which had come to dominate world trade in the eighteenth century, became the cradle of the industrial revolution in the nineteenth. First the textile industry was mechanised and powered by water or by steam engines. Then iron and steel production was revolutionised by the use of coke in blast furnaces, first in the Ironbridge Gorge and then in industrial districts in South Wales, Cumbria, Central Scotland, the North East, Yorkshire and the Black Country. The last name is a clear indication that this early industrialisation caused massive pollution of land, air and water. Coal smoke was perhaps the most widespread pollutant but in areas like Cheshire there were even more devastating pollutants as the infant chemical industry released hydrogen chloride gas into the air, causing acid clouds which killed vegetation for miles around.

Industrialisation did more than revolutionise production. It prompted rapid population growth and even more rapid migration. In 1801, Britain had a population of 10 million, of which 10 per cent lived in towns. By 1901 the population had grown to 25 million of which 77 per cent lived in towns and cities. The rapid growth of large industrial towns and cities was one of the major phenomena of the age, and towns like Birmingham and Manchester grew from small beginnings to a million people or more. It is one of the major paradoxes of the time that mass movement of people into cities where overcrowding and squalor were widespread was actually part of a process where population grew rapidly because mortality rates fell well below fertility rates. Only well into the twentieth century did European fertility rates fall towards mortality rates and population growth reduce. Exactly how and why it did so remains a mystery because it involved new attitudes and lifestyles rather than any technological innovation. So industrialisation involves transformation of whole societies, not just the building of a few factories.

One of the crucial ramifications of industrialisation has been the developments in agriculture and fishing. The application of machines and chemicals has both transformed productivity and increased agriculture's capacity to convert wetland and heathlands to arable use. But it has also dramatically increased impacts on wild plants and animals and begun to contaminate water with nitrates. The increased capacity of modern fishing boats and whalers has severely reduced fish and whale populations, in some cases effectively destroying fisheries and perhaps threatening extinction of some whale species. In partially enclosed seas, the deleterious effects of over-fishing are compounded by pollution from urban and industrial waste.

One threatening impact of industrialisation has been the technologies of mortality control: living standards, attitudes and practices of fertility control have not been able to keep pace. As a result, world population has grown at an ever accelerating rate. For most of human history there have been only a few million hunter-gatherers on Earth. Agricultural societies supported a few hundred million, probably reaching about 600 million in 1500. The century of industrial revolution doubled world population to 1.7 billion in 1890 and growth has continued since then, giving a total population of over 5 billion by 1990. To make matters worse, the current growth rate is two per cent, implying a further doubling in only 35 years. So a world population of ten billion plus is now regarded as probable in the immediate future. Such a growth implies even further extension of agricultural land, more intensive food production and additional environmental impacts. If economic growth is fast enough to continue to increase average living standards, as it has done in the past, growing population multiplied by growing consumption will produce rapidly multiplying impacts on the environment. The prospects must be bleak unless we can think out, and implement, new ways of organising production which have reduced effects on the environment.

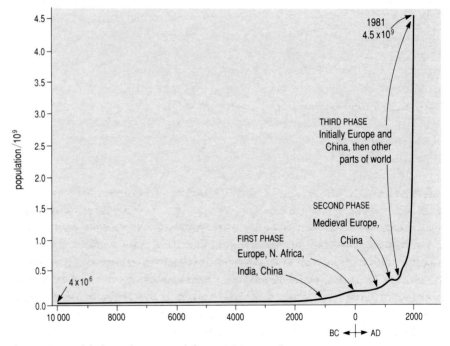

Figure 2.1 *Global population growth from 10,000 BC to the present.*

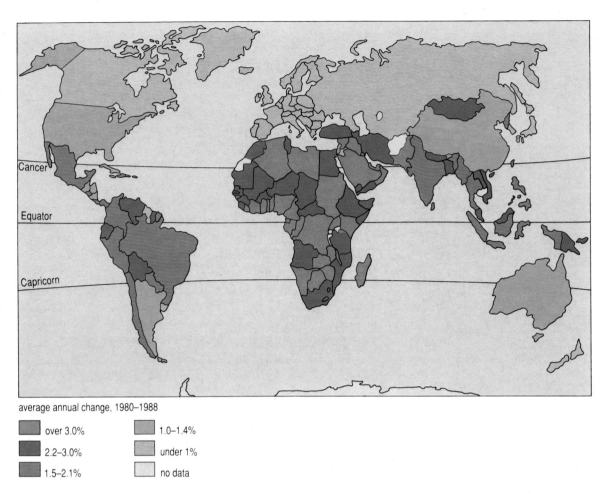

average annual change, 1980–1988

■ over 3.0%		■ 1.0–1.4%	
■ 2.2–3.0%		□ under 1%	
■ 1.5–2.1%		□ no data	

Figure 2.2 *Average annual population growth, 1980–88.*

Unfortunately, the form of deindustrialisation experienced by Britain in the last 20 years is not the harbinger of change. Deindustrialisation has seen a huge fall in the numbers of people employed in manufacturing but output has only fallen slightly. Worse, consumption of manufactured goods has continued to grow, and so have the consequent environmental impacts. The change is that these products are made elsewhere in the world and imported into Britain. To reduce global environmental impacts will require massive changes in methods of production and in the nature of consumption. Such changes are anticipated by the successors of the early environmentalists discussed above.

Population growth rates

Two centuries ago Malthus noted that populations have the potential to increase by 'geometric progression', which in more modern language is described as 'exponential growth'. The distinctive feature of such growth is that because the amount of growth in any period depends on the size of the population at the start of the period, it tends to increase as time passes. Such processes can be expressed as a formula (which is identical to that used by a bank or building society for calculating compound interest), in a graph (where the slope of the graph increases until it rises nearly vertically) or, most simply, through the notion of a **doubling time**.

In a process of exponential growth, the population will double over a given period regardless of the starting point. As it relates to population, there is a useful rule of thumb which shows how percentage growth rate relates to doubling times.

$$\text{DOUBLING TIME} \quad = \quad \frac{70}{\text{PERCENTAGE GROWTH RATE}}$$

So: at one per cent per annum the population will double in

70 YEARS

at two per cent per annum the population will double in

35 YEARS

at three per cent per annum the population will double in

23.33 YEARS

at four per cent per annum the population will double in

17.5 YEARS

Modern environmentalism

Although environmental conservation has had important pioneer thinkers and pressure groups in past centuries, surveys of the media, academic literature, dictionaries and encyclopedias show that there was a decisive change in about 1970. Before that time environmental issues were discussed in a rather fragmented way, often under headings like ecology or conservation. Since then, the term 'environmentalism' (previously used to identify a theoretical position within psychology) has come into common use to identify a new way of thinking about such issues. This new usage stresses the integrated, even holistic, nature of environmental problems and the need to bring about radical social change in order to improve matters. But serious problems remain: exactly how environmental problems are caused is difficult to specify; how society ought to change is even more contentious. A variety of value positions exist and different individuals and organisations may hold views which combine aspects of each. Since values are crucial to policy, it is necessary to construct a clearer picture of the alternatives.

The question would be much easier to handle if, as mass media treatments sometimes imply, the protagonists could be unequivocally identified as exploiters versus environmentalists (now more familiarly known as 'greens'). But in practice, few are willing to admit to being exploiters of environments and most individuals, companies and government departments will pay lip-service to environmental criteria. Even avowed environmentalists are divided between dark (or deep) and light greens. The German Green Party, one of the few environmentalist groups to have held political office, has had intense debates between 'Fundis' (those whose environmental goals were paramount) and 'Realos' (those willing to compromise with mainstream views in order to implement something).

Some of these complexities were already apparent from the nineteenth century issues considered earlier. The argument between Muir (the preservationist) and Pinchot (the conservationist) over the damming of Hetch Hetchy split even the sympathetic Sierra Club because some saw wilderness preservation as more important than municipal water supply and others did not. But even within the two sides in this argument, there were differences of emphasis: Muir tended to argue the case for preservation in terms of the spiritual benefits of 'temples' like Yosemite Valley, and in that respect seems to be a Romantic, but in some of his writings he accepts that nature's interests may override those of humans – for example, accepting that alligators have the right to make a meal of people foolish enough to be caught – and anticipates radical environmentalism. Those in favour of damming Hetch Hetchy, and indeed Thirlmere, seem to have won on the grounds of 'the greatest good of the greatest number', which is the classic position of utilitarianism, but they risked alienating imperialists who believed that such assets should be developed by private interests for profit. All four of the value positions evident in these debates continue to exert an influence, as does one of the oldest positions of all: stewardship.

Attitudes to environment

Environmental imperialism To many in developed societies, whether in mid-nineteenth century Britain or in the USA of Ronald Reagan, the environment existed primarily as a resource. The main aim of society was to exploit resources for profit. In this view, demand for environmental resources would give them economic value, and to the extent that they had value they would be conserved in the sense of being rationed in use.

Utilitarianism or hedonism Born as a challenge to *laissez-faire*, this view argues that the fundamental criterion for preferring one course of action to another is that it should maximise pleasure and minimise pain. While the principle seems clear and democratic, the calculation of pleasure and pain has always been contentious – not least in the modern form of cost-benefit analysis. In practice, pleasure has tended to be replaced by 'demand' and economic calculation to become central.

Stewardship While the Judaeo-Christian tradition has often been seen by environmentalists as encouraging humanity to multiply and to have dominion over Nature, it also produced the concept of stewardship. Here, current occupiers are seen not as owning land or resources but as managing them on behalf of the creator. So they have to manage them responsibly and with an expectation of being held to account. A more modern version of stewardship sees responsibility to future generations rather than to God.

Romanticism Feelings very like those of Wordsworth are still current among people taking countryside recreation. A modern variant on the pantheism of Romanticism is the idea of Gaia. However, Gaia is a more vengeful goddess than the 'Oversoul' of Emerson, and threatens to eliminate the human species unless it mends its ways.

Radical environmentalism In some ways this appears the most coherent position, evident for example in the Greenpeace view that all species have equal rights to survive or in the Green Party critique of industrial society. But in practice there has to be some compromise between people's need for even minimal supplies of food and clothes, and the interests of the natural environments replaced by agriculture. There is also a problem of how to react to non-green people: is it sufficient to drop out of the mainstream and adopt the basic lifestyle of philosopher Arne Naess or should radical environmentalists actively oppose development activities, as do members of 'Earth First!'?

In 1990, when the previously free market inclined Conservative government produced a White Paper on environmental issues, they chose to call it *This Common Inheritance*. The value position it stated was that, while economic growth remained a desirable goal, the current generation had a duty to leave behind it an environment which would not prejudice the prospects of future generations. This is consistent with the concept of stewardship. But to achieve this desirable end in practice requires significant changes to the way economic and political calculations are made. The economic calculations would have to change in two key respects. First, the costs of using stocks of resources or of polluting natural systems would have to be recognised – costs which at present lie outside budgets and are known as 'externalities'. Second, decisions would have to be made in a much longer time-scale if the interests of future generations are to be secured. Such changes would have to extend not only to the budgets of every organisation, but also to the way economic growth is measured. Currently, the concept of Gross National Product (GNP) is used, but it takes no account of environmental assets consumed and even gives credit for the additional economic activity brought about by accidents and disasters. Some economists are currently debating how better measures of economic activity could be constructed, but they face massive inertia which favours existing imperfect measures.

Any change of this magnitude would require determined government action and probably international agreement. To date, successive UK governments have been reluctant to take any action which would be against the short-term interests of industrial or agricultural producers. The UK does have a century's experience of regulation of chemical pollutants, especially by the Alkali Inspectorate, but for much of that time it relied on the concept of 'best practicable means', which were defined in negotiation between inspectors and companies, and which in practice allowed substantial pollution to occur. Recently, EC regulations have moved towards defining 'environmental quality objectives' and fixing emission limits to ensure the objectives are reached. One of the reasons for the move to emission limits is to ensure that all firms meet the same standards and hence to encourage fair competition. The same spirit underlies attempts to move away from a system of legal regulation and fines towards a system based on taxation. The 'polluter pays' principle is now widely quoted, though more rarely implemented, because if polluters really paid the costs of their pollution their production costs would increase. This would leave them unable to compete with overseas producers subject to less stringent controls and might encourage them to move their plant to an overseas location. In practice, most governments have been too concerned about production, profit and employment to risk endangering them through strict environmental regulation or taxation. Such a move probably requires international co-operation.

The development of an international response was a key element of the new environmentalism referred to earlier. In 1970 two new organisations were formed: Greenpeace in Canada and Friends of the Earth in the USA. Each now has branches in many countries. At first their international stance was a response to the issues of nuclear testing and unrestricted whaling. Their goals were both to take direct action to stop these activities and to develop a mass membership to act as a constituency to press governments to change their policies. In the event these groups grew rapidly and were well placed to react to the increasing integration of the world economy and to campaign on major issues like the destruction of rain forests, acid rain, the export of toxic waste and, most recently, global warming. But many other environmentalist groups also grew rapidly in the

1970s and 1980s, from long-established organisations like the Sierra Club and the National Trust, through special interest groups like the Royal Society for the Protection of Birds and its US equivalent, the Audubon Society, to a myriad of other locally-based or special interest groups. The proliferation of disparate environmentalist groups is at best an indication of massive public concern but at worst a confirmation that the environmental movement lacks co-ordinated analyses, priorities and policies. The concentration of these groups in the developed world gives rise to accusations that environmentalism is a self-indulgent response of the affluent.

Rainbow Warrior, sunk in Auckland harbour by French Secret Service agents to prevent Greenpeace protest against nuclear tests in the Pacific.

Greenpeace volunteer blocking outflow pipe of chemical works at Pilkington, Merseyside.

A vital element of the new environmentalism has been the United Nations. It responded quickly to the new mood by holding the Stockholm Conference on the Human Environment in 1972. This led to the 'Declaration on the Human Environment', which identified a fundamental human right to adequate conditions of life in an undegraded environment and consequent duties to protect and improve the environment for future generations. It also led to the establishment of the UN Environmental Program (UNEP) which initiated a monitoring system for global pollution and climate change. UNEP has since been criticised for failing to take a more active lead, but has suffered from limited funding and considerable suspicion from national governments. In the the late 1970s it faced a particular problem as environmental issues were largely ignored by the mass media and politicians preoccupied by recession and unemployment.

In 1983, the UN General Assembly set up the World Commission on Environment and Development under Gro Harlem Brundtland. Its remit was to turn concern into co-operation, to identify long-term environmental issues and ways of tackling them and to propose strategies for sustainable development. Although the concept of sustainable development has proved difficult to define, it is the nearest that the international community has come to an integrated position on environmental issues and their solution. The Commission considered six challenges: growing population, food security, species and ecosystems, energy, industry and urbanisation. They proposed a range of linked policies, legal and institutional changes in their 1987 report *Our Common Future*. This is a long and complex document but within it there is a key element: development should not only be environmentally sustainable, it should also be equitable. This position was justified not only by appeals to human rights but by analyses which showed that many environmental problems are the result of excessive affluence while others result from grinding poverty. In tackling sustainable development in this way, the Commission was reflecting a membership that spoke for the less developed countries as well as more developed countries. In effect, they presented a powerful case for a 'one world' response.

Subsequent reactions have ranged from lip-service to criticisms of particular analyses and proposals. Small wonder when the report proposes that rich and powerful countries should change their behaviour to benefit poor and weak people. However, subsequent international debates over ozone depletion and global warming have confirmed that the industrialised countries need the co-operation of less developed countries if the problems are to be solved. For the first time it can be shown that the industrialised countries have vital interests in the solution of development problems in poor countries as well as environmental problems everywhere. That is the main message of this book.

CHAPTER 3

*Tropical rain forests:
use and abuse*

'I fearlessly assert that here the primaeval forest can
be converted into rich pasture and meadow land, into
cultivated fields, gardens and orchards containing
every variety of produce with half of the labour and,
what is of more importance, in less than half the time
that would be required at home.'
A.R. Wallace, Travels in the Amazon, 1853.

Tropical rain forests play a critical role in regulating the climate and constitute an enormous biological treasurehouse of species. It has been estimated that in Amazonia alone (an area about the size of Australia) the rain forest contains more than 10 per cent of the world's flora and fauna, and the living trees and soil hold over 10 per cent of the carbon dioxide present across the Earth's surface.

Yet conservation of the rain forests is one of the most urgent global environmental issues because they are being destroyed at an alarmingly rapid rate. Estimates of this rate fast become out of date: at the end of the 1980s some sources were claiming that more than 80,000 hectares of forest cover a year were disappearing from those countries lying wholly or mainly within the tropics, including Brazil, Nigeria, Malaysia and Indonesia. Some sources claim that, since 1945, 40 per cent of the world's rain forests have been destroyed and as a result over 50 species of plants and animals become extinct every day.

The last chapter concluded with the essential point that, in the modern environmental movement, the acknowledgement that there exist problems which can be talked of in truly global terms has emphasised the changing nature of the relationship between the more developed and the less developed world. It can now be shown that the more developed world has vital interests in helping to find 'solutions' to these problems. For many environmentalists the disappearance of the tropical forests represents 'an ecological disaster unprecedented in human history' (Jonathon Porritt, 1990), providing the international community with its biggest 'single' problem demanding immediate action.

In this chapter we examine this destruction and its causes, in particular contrasting the use of forest environments by indigenous peoples with their exploitation by modern industrial societies. However, the emphasis is as much on the creation of opportunities for the future balanced development and use of forest resources as dwelling on the dramatic and destructive effects of deforestation. The issues involved are complex, but at the heart is the question of whether, and how, economic development can be reconciled with rain forest conservation. In this, the positive and vital roles to be played by local peoples will be especially highlighted, as well as the policy options open to governments and to the international community.

A study of the Endau Rompin area of lowland tropical rain forest in Peninsular Malaysia focuses on efforts to achieve balanced development in the face of increasing pressures. As one of the last remaining areas of virgin lowland rain forest in Malaysia, Endau Rompin has been of interest to conservationists for over a decade. The participation of the indigenous forest dwellers, the *Orang Jaku*, in these efforts is an important aspect of this study.

◁ **Previous page**
Burning forest in the vicinity of Rio Branco, Brazil,
to enlarge cattle ranches.

The extent to which environmentalists in Malaysia are able to achieve the sustainable management of the tropical forest is used as a 'benchmark' for exploring the wider issues of deforestation in regions as far apart as Amazonia and India. Can the ecological catastrophe so widely predicted be averted? What roles do the principal 'actors' – governments of less developed countries, land owners, the industrialised nations, the multinational companies, pressure groups, local peoples – have in this unfolding tragedy? Are there viable policy options available now to ensure the long-term survival of the rain forests?

An exploitable resource

The tremendous riches of the rain forest – the impressively tall trees, the lush vegetation, the diversity of species of flora and fauna – have long been taken to represent great fertility by successive generations of explorers and scientists. The British naturalist, Alfred Russell Wallace (1823–1913), spent several years exploring the Amazon region and envisaged a resource to be exploited, although he was clearly thinking in terms of soil fertility rather than the products of the forest.

This dangerously false assumption, shared by most visitors to Amazonia until the middle of the twentieth century, based as it was purely upon observation rather than hard scientific analysis, has been one of the principal causes of the current environmental threat to the rain forests. It is simply an illusion that large trees and luxuriant green growth indicate a fertile soil. There is considerable variability of soils in the Amazon basin, but most are millions of years old and have had their nutrients long since washed out of them by rainfall. Even the most fertile soils lack the fertility and nutrient retaining capacity of more recently formed soils in temperate regions of the world, as in the UK for example.

Many governments in the less developed countries also regard their forests as resources to be exploited, comparing their situation to that which led to the clearance of forests in the temperate zone during the industrial development of the 'north'. Particularly notable among these has been the Brazilian Government, which began encouraging settlement and forest clearance for agriculture in Amazonia during the years of military dictatorship in the early 1970s, under the rubric 'Operation Amazon'. The objective was to 'flood the Amazon with civilisation' by persuading peasant settlers to come to the region, purportedly to ease population pressure in Brazil's overcrowded coastal periphery. The incentive was the prospect of unlimited fertile land, of 'land without men for men without land'. Construction of the trans-Amazon highway was begun in 1970 to facilitate this process of colonisation.

The forest canopy: Extractive Reserve in Upper Jurua, Acre, Brazil.

Migrant 'slash and burn' cultivators burning forest to grow subsistence crops in the vicinity of Rio Branco, Brazil.

The whole enterprise was grossly misguided and doomed to failure. Clearing the forest by burning does return most of the nutrients held in the vegetation to the soil, but most of the soil has little retentive capacity for these nutrients. So within a few seasons of growing crops, even with the addition of artificial fertilisers, soil nutrients are exhausted and the land has to be converted to very low grade cattle pasture or abandoned altogether. Peasant farmers move on to a new area of forest and the process is repeated.

We shall be taking a longer look at Amazonia later in the chapter. The box overleaf provides some of the more depressing statistics in the story of the rain forests as a resource to be exploited. The last item in the box serves to underline a fundamental element in the debate about the use and abuse of the rain forests: the ownership of land. This is particularly the case in the Amazon region, but is crucial whether we are looking at a large scale or on a smaller, more local scale, as in the case of the Endau Rompin area. Land reform, sustainability and equity are interconnected themes in the unfolding story as we attempt to shift the emphasis from short-term, economic exploitation to long-term 'wise use' of resources and conservation.

▶ *The devastating effects of deforestation in what was formerly a mangrove forest in Haiti.*

Rain forest factsheet

- With just two per cent of the world's population, Japan takes some 40 per cent of the mahogany from the rain forests.

- Huge multinationals, like Mitsubishi, are orchestrating massive logging operations in Malaysia, Indonesia, , Central Africa and the Amazon.

- In the 1950s four-fifths of the Caribbean island of Haiti were covered by forests; by 1990 this had been reduced to one-twentieth through logging and charcoal burning.

- Charcoal burning is a by-product of logging and has become a boom industry in many regions, especially in Amazonia where it provides fuel for the smelting of pig iron. Iron ore is present in large quantities and mining companies have moved in with massive investments.

- One of the largest international projects in Amazonia is the Carajas Iron Ore scheme, jointly financed by the World Bank, the EC and Japan. This will convert an area of forest the size of France to industrial and agricultural use, with the production of pig iron for export to make cars in Japan and the EC.

- The rate of forest destruction in Brazil was estimated, in 1990, to be around 42,000 square kilometres a year – an area greater than the Netherlands.

- Paragominas in Brazil has been called 'the saw mill capital of the world' – 500 mills handle 5,000 trees a day.

- Forest fires (called *queimadas* in the Amazon) release at least two billion tonnes of carbon dioxide per year into the atmosphere, increasing global warming.

- Since 'Operation Amazon' was launched, land speculation has resulted in more than 600,000 square kilometres passing into private hands, mostly in the form of large cattle ranches.

Endau Rompin – an uncertain future?

The stark information presented in the box above makes for depressing reading. Understandably perhaps, many environmentalists are taking a highly alarmist stance on the widespread destruction. Friends of the Earth have been at the forefront of pressure groups campaigning to increase awareness, and to bring home to governments and development agencies in particular the need for action now rather than later.

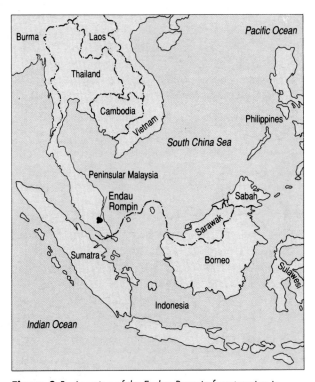

Figure 3.1 *Location of the Endau Rompin forest region in Peninsular Malaysia.*

In the Endau Rompin rain forest of Malaysia conservationists have been making concerted efforts for over 10 years to protect the region entirely from logging activities and other intensive exploitation. Prominent amongst these has been the Malayan Nature Society, which has organised a series of expeditions into the area, including a highly publicised Heritage Expedition aimed at increasing awareness among the Malaysian public. The organiser of the expedition, Heah Hock Heng, explains its aims:

'The Society set up the expedition to provide basic information about this area which is large but very little known. Until we actually had scientists going into the forest and starting to take an inventory of what is there, it was just a big blank on the map. I think new discoveries are constantly being made. The harder you look the more discoveries you will find.'

Heah Hock Heng of the Malayan Nature Society.

Although Malaysia has substantial tracts of rain forest remaining and is attempting to pursue a relatively progressive path to industrial and economic development, extensive exploitation of forest resources remains a controversial issue in a number of areas. Most notable is Sarawak, one of the largest states in Malaysia covering 48,000 square kilometres, of which approximately 70 per cent is officially rain forest. The majority of the population of 1.4 million are tribal people who rely on the natural resources of the forests for their livelihoods. The problem is that virtually all Sarawak's forests are now registered timber concessions, even though they are tribal homelands supposedly protected by law. This means that logging continues apace, with Japan as one of the main consumers of the cheap hardwoods.

The Penan forest peoples have been actively campaigning against the loggers, in particular by forming human barricades across the logging roads. Here is an extract from a plea, distributed by Friends of the Earth:

'We appeal to all friends within and outside Malaysia to help stop the logging on our customary land. Only our forests can guarantee survival.

Our people have no choice but to blockade the logging activities that trespassed on our land. We have not committed any wrongs or crimes. It is the loggers who damaged our land, crops, burial grounds and who pollute our rivers.

We demand that the Malaysian Government should immediately take steps to stop logging on our land and forest.'

Plea from the Penan Peoples of Sarawak, 'signed' by Depe Alat, Bungan and Pelutan, sponsored by Sarawak FoE, 1990.

The displacement of indigenous peoples in the rain forests is a familiar theme, not least in Amazonia; but in Endau Rompin the conservationists are working with the forest dwellers, the Orang Jaku, in their efforts to promote the sustainable use of the forest and demonstrate to government and development agencies what might be achieved with longer-term objectives in mind. The Orang Jaku have developed a harmonious relationship with the forest over millennia, living off its products and practising shifting cultivation on a sustainable basis. Some of the products which they have traditionally collected, such as rattan, can now provide them with a source

Making a rattan chair, using raw materials produced on a sustainable basis in Endau Rompin, Malaysia.

of income and there is potential for developing such activities further. The main issue to be confronted is this: how can the tropical forest survive in the face of more intensive forms of exploitation like logging, or compete with alternative forms of land use such as rubber and oil palm plantations?

Of a rich ecosystem and biodiversity

The key to appreciating the richness of the tropical rain forest, as it exists today in Endau Rompin, lies in understanding how the complex ecosystem functions and how important is the concept of biodiversity. The notion of the ecosystem as a useful means of explaining the complex interrelationships and interdependencies of living organisms was discussed in Chapter 1 (see pages 13–14). Biodiversity is simply a term to define the great range and diversity of species found in a virgin rain forest. Chee Yoke Ling of Malaysian Friends of the Earth states:

> 'I think there's a lot of emotive appeal in the tropical rain forest issue because people can relate very easily with trees – with flora and fauna – with the diversity, because it is so concrete an example of nature. People can relate to it very easily, so that partly accounts for the public concern when the destruction takes place.'

The continuous functioning of the rain forest ecosystem is directly related to how the relatively poor soils are able to support mature forest by efficient nutrient cycling. This means that rain forest trees are able to grow on poor soils because they are extremely efficient at recapturing the nutrients released by the decomposition of organic matter on the surface of the soil. This depends upon the rapid decomposition of *litter* (leaves etc.) and what are called mycorrhizal associations between tree roots and fungi that enable trees to mop up nutrients quickly. Termites are particularly important agents in the decomposition of dead wood.

Tropical forests contain a multitude of species of flora and fauna, many of which are rare, so that species new to science are routinely found by scientific expeditions, like those organised by the Malayan Nature Society. Detailed study of the entire range of species has not been achieved in Endau Rompin, nor for that matter in most other tropical forests, but an indication of what might be found is given by the huge total of 820 tree species identified in a research plot of one half of a square kilometre at Pasoh in Malaysia. Animal diversity, especially insect diversity, is also almost incomprehensibly large in such forests.

Statistics can certainly vary depending on which scientist you are talking to, but there is an overwhelming consensus amongst botanists, ecologists and zoologists on the great significance of the biodiversity of the rain forests as presenting one of the strongest arguments for their conservation and long-term management. Not least of the points to be made concerns the potential of tropical plants to be used for medicinal purposes. Some scientists optimistically predict that at least 1,400 tropical plant species offer potential against various forms of cancer.

Of course such predictions are speculative and much more research is needed. The question is who takes the responsibility for such research. Most often it is the multinational pharmaceutical companies. The amount of genetic material coming out of the Amazon region is estimated at several million dollars worth a year, but who benefits from this? The indigenous tribes who have actually managed the forests on a sustainable basis and have 'unlocked their secrets' are having to fight to protect their very livelihoods, as in the case of the Penan of Sarawak, and usually this is a losing battle.

Part of the forest region of Endau Rompin being proposed as a National Park by the Malayan Nature Society.

In Endau Rompin there are indications that conservationists, in conjunction with the authorities, can work in partnership with the Orang Jaku to ensure that the area is entirely protected from intensive commercial exploitation. The Malayan Nature Society is talking in terms of designating the region as a National Park, with 'buffer zones' around the protected areas where 'low intensity' exploitation could be carried on. There are areas of logged forest where seedlings are present that could enable the forest to recover, but such a process takes at least 70 years. Taking a long-term view, this could provide the basis for sustainable management if market conditions are right, but the pressures for cheap products and quick profits make such an option very difficult to pursue.

The problem with creating a national park, which recognises the fragile nature of the tropical forest ecosystem and its importance in terms of biodiversity, is that such environmentally protectionist policies tend to be exclusive. Does this mean that the remainder of the forest must be considered as lost? In the long run such a policy may not be in the best interests of the local peoples either, since the forest has to be viewed as a living entity and not something to be preserved. This is the crux of the dilemma: on the one hand forests must be utilised to produce some form of economic return, yet on the other hand utilisation can lead to destruction. Chee Yoke Ling addresses this dilemma:

> 'Conservation is viewed by some people to mean let's just set aside the area and keep it as it is. I think in the rain forest we cannot divorce the resources of the forest from the people who live in the forest, or who live on the outskirts of the forest with a will to depend on the forest resources. So we cannot support a system where you create areas where suddenly very sensitive areas should be no touch. We cannot ignore the rights of forest people all over the world who have traditionally used the forest, in many cases very sustainably, and we need to take into account those users. So conservation is really conservation for ecological purposes as well as to see how those resources can serve the need of rural populations and forest dwellers; but it needs to be done in such a way that overexploitation again by the same group of people does not take place.'

Use and abuse – a global dilemma?

The protectionist approach to rain forest conservation has been widely espoused by environmentalists in the developed world. Graphic illustrations of falling trees and vast areas blackened by fire, and stark figures recording the numbers of species lost, have tended to skew the emphasis on what actually needs to be done. Many environmentalists see people as the problem when they can be part of the solution.

Even when an important individual emerges, as in the case of Chico Mendes, ecologist and union leader of the rubber tappers in the remote Brazilian Amazon region of Acre, who was murdered in 1989, a distorted 'media hyped' view is likely to emerge. Mendes has been portrayed as an 'ecological martyr' to focus world attention on the destruction of the forests. We in the more developed world have been encouraged to fight to save the trees; what is overlooked is that Mendes was a radical labour leader, founder of the Forest People's Alliance, who was involved in a battle to save the livelihoods of the indigenous Indian tribes. The connecting factor is that their livelihoods depend upon trees.

In all the discussions about causes and effects of rain forest destruction it is the social dimension which is most often the least appreciated; yet an understanding of the social processes involved and a recognition of the importance of a stable social base in the forests are both vital. The forests cannot survive without people, but they have to be used and managed in a sustainable way that ensures the natural resources, the forests' environmental capital, are conserved and replenished on a long-term basis.

So is the issue of 'use and abuse' of the rain forests a matter of global concern, to be dealt with by the international community, and if this is the case, how and on what basis? Or is it primarily the responsibility of sovereign states, like Brazil and Malaysia, to provide the necessary legislative framework for containing development and promoting 'wise' use and management? These two questions imply that there may well be a dilemma of global proportions – there are after all continuing expressions of international concern about the disappearance of the forests – but that there exists no single or simple set of solutions. As this chapter has already set out to establish, the issues are varied and complex. Most interested observers regard the Amazon as 'the big problem', but how will the problem in the Amazon have an impact on, say, future utilisation policies in Asia or Africa?

Amazonia – a special case?

It is understandable that so much attention has been focused on the Amazonian rain forest. Despite the rate at which the forests are being cleared, vast expanses still remain (see Figure 3.2) and it is the sheer scale of the whole region which leaves its impress upon us. We tend to associate the region just with Brazil, although the forests do extend into Peru, Colombia and Venezuela. Unequivocally, the Brazilian Government has had a major part to play in the tale of destruction.

Deforestation along a new road in Amazonia, Peru.

The facts presented in the box on page 42 place an emphasis on the role played by the developed world. Certainly, schemes such as the Carajas Iron Ore Project have been funded by the World Bank, along with the European Community and Japan, but with the full complicity of the Brazilian Government. An increasing number of environmentalists are coming to recognise that the principal culprits of the destruction of the Amazonian forests are to be found inside Brazil, especially amongst the military and the industrial elite who formed alliances during the years of dictatorship. Their

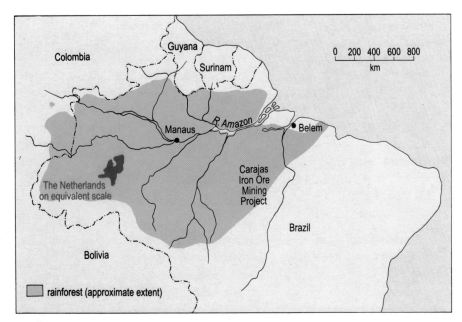

Figure 3.2 *The extent of the Amazonian rain forest in Latin America.*

large-scale development plans and doctrines of national security still act as guiding principles despite moves towards democracy and greater political stability in recent years.

The massive programme of colonisation that was part of Operation Amazon served to replicate, in Amazonia, the highly inequitable forms of land holding that dominate much of Latin America, the vast estates or *latifundios*. As explained already, the forest has been an economic disaster for most of the peasant 'settlers'. Over 50 per cent of the cleared land has now been abandoned as unproductive, with the consequent soil erosion producing great swathes of waste land, never to be reclaimed. Because of the poor soil quality virtually the whole of the territory is uneconomic for modern agriculture or pastoralism, yet with the fiscal incentives available from the Government, land speculation has been fervently pursued, predominantly by cattle ranchers.

The ranches, mostly operating at a 'carrying capacity' of less than one animal per acre, have also been an economic as well as an ecological disaster. They have only survived because of huge government subsidies, guaranteeing large profits for the landowners, and the 'unholy alliance' between successive governments and the very powerful cattle ranchers union, the UDR. So enormous sums of money have at the same time been fuelling the national debt, lining the pockets of the new landowners and producing forest destruction on a massive scale.

Cattle ranch in cleared forest, Rio Branco, Brazil. Although huge areas of forest have been turned into pasture to raise cattle, the Amazon is a net importer of beef.

Land speculation, specifically in the form of cattle ranching, then, has been a greater cause of deforestation in Amazonia than any form of production. Large-scale projects, and commercial logging (which throughout the tropical rain forests is directly responsible for only around 20 per cent of the deforestation) are, of course, also significant factors; but the main issue concerns the responsibility for taking action to check the destruction, ultimately with the aim of changing the development tack altogether. In this, the international community has arguably less of a role to play than the Brazilian Government.

A number of Amazon 'experts' take this view. Despite the huge debt repayments with which the country is saddled, Brazil is an autonomous state and a major economic power in the less developed countries. Amazonia may comprise around 60 per cent of Brazil's territory, but only 12 million people live there (less than 10 per cent of the total population of 130 million, according to the latest census of 1983). International factors are clearly not insignificant, but 'solutions' like waiving the national debt or negotiating debt-for-nature swaps (where 'bad debts' are sold off at a discounted value in exchange for 'shares' in an environmental 'commodity' like forests) will not 'save' the rain forest, according to some experts.

Such options may have a greater relevance in other regions of the tropics but in the Amazon region it is apparent that two policy issues are dominant: land ownership and the development model. The need for land reform is paramount, but it is also political dynamite. The power of vested commercial interests remains very strong.

In its moves towards greater democratisation, the Brazilian Government of the early 1990s has introduced some new policies, claiming that the rate of destruction has fallen sharply, 'from 35,000 square miles in 1987 to just 1,900 in 1990' according to the Minister of the Environment in February 1991; but these have yet to incorporate major changes to the way land is owned and managed. If political stability is achieved in the longer term and there is greater participation in decision-making, particularly on the part of the forest peoples (as demanded, for example, by the Forest Peoples' Alliance), then significant reforms may come. But it is a big 'if'.

The issue of an appropriate model of development clearly extends beyond Brazil's frontiers. It is a basic topic to which we return in detail in Chapters 9 and 10 and it represents an underlying theme of the whole book. It raises the taxing question of the extent to which any sovereign state, and particularly one in the less developed world, has the 'power' to determine its own destiny within the complex web of interrelationships that make up the global economic system. That is not to say that Brazil has no choice in how 'development' should occur, but that there are inevitable constraints beyond the realms of political expediency and social choice, however they may be seen to operate.

An end to large-scale 'development' schemes in Amazonia and a move to 'local', small-scale ones would clearly be beneficial to the rain forests; but in economic terms are not big projects such as major hydroelectric power schemes a more efficient way to utilise development funds? Protagonists have long contested that huge 'trickle down' projects just do not work. The only ones to benefit are the developers. If we journey half way round the world to the Narmada Valley in India we can examine such arguments in a different locational context.

What forms of development?

The Narmada River scheme is set to become the world's largest hydroelectric power and irrigation complex. The project involves the building of 30 major dams, 135 medium-sized dams and 3,000 small dams over a period of 50 years. It is designed to irrigate 20,000 square kilometres in the drought-prone states of Gujarat and Madhya Pradesh, provide drinking water for the whole region and generate 500 million megawatts of electricity. It represents the grand development scheme *par excellence* and much of the estimated cost of around 40 billion dollars will be met by the World Bank.

It has also produced India's first nationwide environmental protest movement, bringing together campaigners for peasants' rights, fishermen, the urban poor and other groups who see the scheme as 'an environmental catastrophe, a technological dinosaur and flagrant social injustice' (*The Guardian*, 25 January 1991). The dams, when completed, will displace more than 200,000 people, submerge 2,000 square kilometres of fertile land and 1,500 square kilometres of forest. In fact the forest loss will be greater than these 'official' estimates, because many people will be relocated into forest watershed regions, worsening soil erosion problems.

The Sardar Sarowar Dam site on the Narmada River in Gujarat State will be the second largest concrete gravity dam in the world.

In support of the project the Government has used some powerful propaganda messages: 'The Narmada Dams will provide irrigation and drinking water to prospective populations of nearly 40 million' and 'India must be self-sufficient in food to avoid going round the world with a begging bowl.'

The nub of the opponents' case is this: environmental damage would be minimised with hundreds of local irrigation projects which could do the same job at a fraction of the cost. Poor farmers and agriculture in general will both lose out because the whole scheme will benefit more intensive farming methods, encouraging those who are already prosperous to grow more cash crops, leaving peasant farmers upstream with even less water. This has been the result of large-scale development schemes the world over. What sets out to be a development to benefit everyone in fact only benefits the already wealthy and the developers themselves. Environmentalists argue that this is the antithesis of sustainable development, a primary objective of which is greater equity, not more inequity. This theme is picked up in the next chapter on the issue of food security.

In Cameroon the threat to the forests is of a different dimension, although the 'development ethos' remains as a fairly constant factor, representing a dominating perspective from the industrialised world. It is the last country in Western Africa to exploit its forests, which cover 1.4 million square kilometres or more than 50 per cent of the land. The political will to protect the forest and to use sustainable methods does appear to exist. The Government aims to safeguard about 20 per cent in its Tropical Forest Action Plan and ban the export of logs by 1995, as part of a programme with the World Bank and the FAO. This is an encouraging stance to adopt.

The reality is that demands for timber (as firewood) are growing rapidly, from within the country, from neighbouring Nigeria and (for export) from an increasing number of companies. By mid-1990 over 150 companies had been awarded licensing concessions to log, of which only 23 were Cameroon based and most of these were European funded. Given such pressures it is extremely doubtful that Cameroon can afford the sort of forestry service needed to carry out its policy requirements. For one thing, illegal logging is commonplace throughout the tropics.

Large-scale logging is perceived as the major threat, but western ideas on conservation could also threaten traditional livelihoods in the forests. In 1986 the Korup National Park (see Figure 3.3) was designated to give legal protection against cutting down the forest. Now a scheme is being proposed, with aid from the European Community and elsewhere, to protect 1,250 square kilometres of jungle as a sort of ecological heritage area. The problem is that a number of villages will have to be 'relocated' for the scheme to succeed in ecological terms: the rain forest is to be saved for posterity – no one will be able to use the area for the traditional purpose of hunting.

▲ **The Korup National Park, Cameroon, West Africa.**

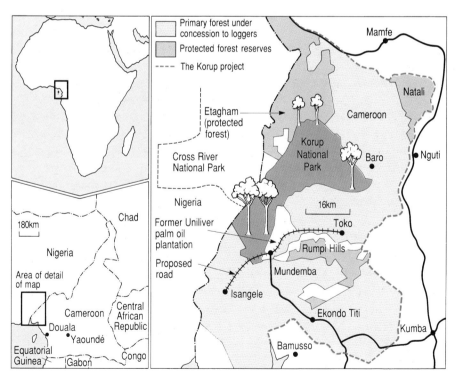

Figure 3.3 *Location of the Korup National Park.*

Sustainable use – a feasible option?

The brief journey we have taken through some of the threatened forests in the tropics has certainly demonstrated the complex web of interrelationships which exist. Some principal themes are recurrent, however. Predominant are the responsibilities of the more developed nations. The odds really are stacked against the poorer countries. The global economic system, whose generating force is industrial capitalism, is not about issues of equity, fair distribution or social justice. It is about the use and exploitation of the Earth's resources for short-term gain or profit. Logging is a prime example. It also inevitably prescribes the model of development for the less developed world that ensures the continuance of economic dependency in a relentless and often ruthless spirit of neo-colonialism. The ethos is: what is in it for us and how will we benefit? This sentiment underpins almost all programmes of aid from the more developed to the less developed world.

Yet, as we have shown, governments in less developed countries are by no means blameless when it comes to exploiting the riches of the forests. This is particularly the case in the Amazon region. Corruption and the undemocratic use of power by elites makes the burden for the poor doubly hard to bear. Some reforms can only come from within these countries and land reform has to be at the top of the agenda. Even where there appears to be an enlightened government, as in Cameroon, the pressures stemming from the unequal relationship described in the previous paragraph continue to imperil their natural resources.

A recurrent theme has also been that of sustainability. The general concept of sustainable development as an 'option for the future' is examined in Chapters 9 and 10. In the case of the rain forests there are some signs that the wisdom of sustainable use is gaining ground. There is, after all, nothing new in the concept of 'sustained yield': indigenous forest dwellers have been practising just such an art for generations. In Endau Rompin, for instance, there is some cause to be optimistic in the participation of the Orang Jaku in future management schemes, and the concept of Extractive Reserves, first developed in the Amazon, is beginning to be used elsewhere.

The challenge for sustainable development in the tropical rain forests is to 'solve' the conflict between resource exploitation, spurred on by the lure of short-term economic and/or political gain, and resource conservation with its message of long-term 'wise' economic use and management, which enhances rather than prejudices the livelihoods of the forest peoples. The question remains for the time being as to the balance of responsibilities for taking up this challenge between the more developed and the less developed world. Is there a tendency in the environmental debate to put too much

A Japanese sponsored agro-forestry farm at Tomeacu, Paragominas, Brazil – a very successful example of sustainable farming, harvesting cocoa.

blame on the former? The more developed countries are clearly cast as the traditional villains of the piece, but as the less developed countries 'develop' where does one end and the other start?

The following box provides a starting point, at least for meeting some of the challenges:

Achieving a sustainable future for the rain forests

- Waiving the debt for less developed nations, negotiating 'debt-for-nature' swaps: any debt renegotiations would require strings to be attached. How could countries be made accountable for their actions in the environment? What sanctions could be operated?

- Boycotting tropical hardwoods: Friends of the Earth have been running an international campaign for a number of years. What about the major markets like the Japanese? And what of the impact on traditional livelihoods of indigenous peoples?

- Ensuring social and political rights for the forest peoples: a high priority which must accompany moves towards democratisation and greater political stability in a number of countries.

- Marketing sustainably produced rain forest products which take account of traditional patterns of trade and fully involve the indigenous peoples.

- Setting up an international convention for tropical forests in a similar manner to that which already operates for the oceans. What about the issue of sovereignty?

- Seeing the forests as a *sustainable resource* in terms of their *total economic value*: this would include both 'use' and 'non-use' values. Direct use values would include watershed protection and carbon fixation (in relation to global warming), as well as the resources themselves. Non-use values relate to *existence value*, that is the value environmentalists place on conserving tropical forests regardless of any direct use in the present or the future.

'I think the reconciliation can only take place if societies as a whole in all tropical rain forest countries realise that the rain forest, or any other resources, or the environment as a whole, has to be conserved, for all reasons, not just because we want to have a beautiful environment, but for very sound economic planning and to be able to sustain our population as long a term as possible. Then, if that awareness exists, people and institutions in a country will accordingly make demands from politicians. So that people who want to come into political power have to show that they abide by that same principle. So we need to build that awareness as a society; then we dictate the political development.'

Chee Yoke Ling, Malaysian Friends of the Earth, 1990

CHAPTER 4

Feeding the five billion

'The thick forest we had before had gone. The reason
why the forest had gone was that the number of people
who settled here increased and the Europeans started to
rule us. People became relaxed and happy because there
were no more wars with the warlike nomads. Also the
amount of farming increased and within three months
one farmer can destroy many trees. During the dry
season the trees are burnt down until all the forest had
gone completely.'

Chief of Garadoume village.

Agriculture is one of the major ways in which human societies affect the environment. All kinds of agriculture displace natural species and some replace whole ecosystems, notably through deforestation. More recently, agricultural machinery and chemicals have increased the severity of environmental impacts. Yet we should not exaggerate the extent of agricultural land: only a little over one-tenth of the Earth's land surface is used for crops and a further quarter for pasture. Given the rapid population growth described in Chapter 2, future years are likely to see further extensions and intensification of agricultural use and environmental impact. This raises major questions about how agricultural production can be improved without excessive environmental impact. This is one of the main questions considered in this chapter.

However, before the issue of future policy can be sensibly tackled, we must first consider the inability of current agriculture to feed the human population. Recent famines in Bangladesh in 1974–5 and the Sahel (the countries on the southern edge of the Sahara desert) in 1968–73, 1984–5 and 1989–90 are a stark reminder that food production and distribution are not adequate to reach the poorest of the poor. Indeed, these famines are only a sporadic worsening of a situation which leaves hundreds of millions of people underfed. The fact that Europe and the USA suffer from overproduction of food and that their governments are trying to reduce agricultural output serves to dramatise the inadequacies of the current system.

However, it would be premature to conclude, as so often happens, that the solution to the two problems is to transfer the rich countries' surpluses to the hungry. Not only have developed countries proved unwilling to sustain such transfers on an adequate scale, but they have been shown to damage less developed producers by lowering crop prices. Beyond this, the commonsense 'solution' suggests that the developed countries are producing food in a desirable way and that less developed countries are incapable of feeding themselves. This chapter will show that neither of these is the case. A lasting solution to the problems of surplus, famine and environmental impact needs to be based on an understanding of the real causes of the problems, which are social and economic.

To identify the nature and causes of agricultural problems, we will start by looking at a typical 'problem area' in Niger, then widen the focus to show how the current system of agricultural production and trade works to produce the current problems. More optimistically, we will argue that the past and present performance of agriculture gives every hope of feeding current and future populations – providing that governments, especially in developed countries, can be persuaded to change their policies on agriculture and agricultural trade.

Previous page
Like other countries in the Sahel, Niger has been badly hit by drought and desertification.

Agriculture, desertification and famine in Niger

The former French colony of Niger lies north of Nigeria and spans semi-arid and desert zones. It has a population of eight million and an area five times that of the UK. It is one of the poorest countries in the world, with a GNP per capita of less than $500. More than three-quarters of its population are directly dependent on agriculture. In the past most of the country was given over to nomadic pastoralism with settled agriculture only in wetter parts of the south.

Millet is one of the staple crops of semi-arid areas like Niger.

The village of Garadoume, in the Majjia valley of central Niger, lies near the northern margin of cultivation. Staple crops are sorghum, millet and cowpea. These crops can be grown with as little as 300 mm of rain – half the rainfall of East Anglia. Like other Sahelian countries, Niger experiences great variation in rainfall from year to year and since 1970 many more years have fallen below the long-term average than above. To further compound the problem, much of the rain falls in a small number of violent storms and there is a long dry season. The problems for farmers are exacerbated by the hot Harmattan wind which sometimes blows from the Sahara, sandblasting young plants. The heavy rainstorms have eroded the soil on the steep sides of the valley, bringing sand and gravel into the better fields of the valley bottom. The whole process is cumulative: soil erosion reduces crop growth, which increases exposure to driving rain and promotes further soil erosion.

Former nomads, the Fulani tribe was forcibly settled after drought

In some areas these problems are compounded by the presence of Fulani people who lost their herds in the drought years and have to grow crops to survive. The result for the people is an insecure supply of staple foods and low incomes because of an inability to sell surplus crops. The result for the environment is increased soil erosion and the threat of desertification.

In spite of this growth in the population, it remains by international standards extremely sparse. Like other parts of Africa, Niger suffers from labour shortages. The kinds of response to difficult and semi-arid environments which have occurred in India or China could not occur here. Terraces or irrigation systems both require much more labour input than is available, except where international projects have brought modern technology to the Niger Valley. In areas like Garadoume, the shortage of labour is compounded by the migration of many young men to Niamey or to Nigerian cities in search of higher wages. So low agricultural productivity is both a cause and a result of migration and environmental degradation.

▲ *In the dry season, the only source of water is from pits dug in the river bed. Water collection is backbreaking work, entirely done by women. In the background are the trees of one of the successful windbreaks.*

Local responses

A variety of improvement projects exist in the Majjia Valley, which combine to show how semi-arid envirorments can be more effectively managed. Most of these involve outside agencies, but in every case these agencies are working with and through local communities. In contrast to an earlier approach in which outside agencies attempted to impose capital intensive solutions like dams or mechanisation, these projects recognise that better management will only become permanent if it is taken up by the locals. The aim is to provide wages in the short term and to create a longer-term source of income.

A combination of banks, tree plantations and terraces prevent soil erosion and create favourable sites for crops. They also increase water infiltration and so increase the amounts of ground water. The additional storage of water underground keeps springs flowing during the dry season and so provides improved water supply for people and animals and even some limited irrigation on the valley floor.

But the second serious problem is the wind. The only way to combat this is to plant belts of trees. Trees provide shelter for distances equal to

▼ *Members of the mwethia – women's self-help group – in Kenya build terraces to slow runoff and increase water penetration.*

10 times their height. A project funded by CARE started 15 years ago shows the problems and the benefits. The tree belts shading nearby crops compete for water, so lowering yields for some distance. However, further away, the shelter increases yields so total yield can increase. The choice of species and spacing is vital and is being researched by scientists so that future shelter belts can be even more efficient.

> 'The crops that are planted where we have the trees grow better than compared to the places where we don't have the trees. That was how we realised the benefits. When the trees are fully grown, people use some of the branches for cooking and the fallen leaves act as fertilisers on our land.'
>
> Chief of Garadoume village.

Near Garadoume, the trees pose a different problem: who should benefit from this valuable new timber supply? The answer worked out locally is that a share goes to the farmer on whose land the tree grew but the majority of the value goes to the wood marketing co-operative to fund further improvements. In the process the women of the village gain because they can buy firewood rather than spending hours cutting it, and the environment gains because trees elsewhere can develop without suffering the attention of firewood collectors.

An additional approach to agricultural improvement is by breeding improved varieties of crops. The staples in Niger are sorghum and millet but unlike maize, which is increasingly grown in less arid areas of Africa, little work has been done on selection for better yield and disease resistance. The International Crop Research Institute for the Semi-arid Tropics (ICRISAT) has a research station at Niamey in Niger where promising progress is being made, though there are formidable pest problems. Intercropping of certain trees and shrubs with millet is another way of conserving soil and providing animal feed. Experiments are also being carried out on cash crops, but these link to the wider social causes of the problems for the Sahel.

The wider context

The photographs and TV coverage we see of countries in the Sahel and the fact that we see them in drought periods, like 1968–74 and the mid-1980s, suggest that the causes of famine and desertification lie in the climate and the inability of subsistence farmers and pastoralists to adjust. These factors are real, but a further cause is the way that countries like Niger have been incorporated into world agricultural trade.

Since 1945, subsistence production in Niger has been disrupted by two kinds of production for export. The number of grazing animals and the land

The peanut is Niger's main export, but has created serious problems of soil exhaustion.

devoted to peanut growing roughly quadrupled in 20 years. So the drought of the late 1960s found an environment under much greater pressure than had any earlier drought. Why did this happen?

Oddly enough, the major cause was the USA's success in exporting soya beans into Europe for oil production. The French Government set out to resist this by expanding the output of peanuts from its African colonies. Niger had only a short history of peanut growing but a French Government campaign was able to double the amount of land planted with peanuts in three years – from 142,000 hectares in 1954 to 302,000 in 1957. Even after Niger gained its independence, the adoption of improved varieties and methods developed by a Senegalese research station kept yields increasing and spread peanuts ever further north. Although the Government of Niger tried to limit the spread, many farmers obtained over half their income from peanuts and were reluctant to give it up. Indeed, Niger came to depend on peanuts for two-thirds of its exports and seemed in the 1960s to be a shining example of the Green Revolution.

Unfortunately, there were a number of problems which were brutally exposed by drought. First, most farmers had planted peanuts on their fallow land so that they could maintain output of food crops. Second, the peanut is a very demanding crop because its high yield of fat requires a high level of soil nutrients. Third, many farmers lacked the cash needed to buy the recommended levels of fertiliser. The consequence was a decline in soil fertility and hence yields, not only of peanuts but also of staples. The increasing difficulty of maintaining output was made even more problematic by falling prices. The French Government had set a high price and shielded Niger from fluctuations in world price, but in 1965 Niger and 17 other African countries became associate members of the EC and the price support was phased out. So peanut production had destabilised Niger's farming without producing a reliable source of income.

The process of boom and bust development was even more extreme in the case of livestock. Once again French development capital took a hand, installing abattoirs, refrigerated transport and even establishing experimental ranches. Numbers of cattle increased and pastoralists moved further into the desert fringe, encouraged by the increasing number of wells being installed. Once again, incomes rose but the resilience of the system declined. The drought of the late 1960s cut staple crop output by 50 per cent and cattle numbers by 40 per cent, leading to impoverishment and famine. The wetter years of the late 1970s improved matters somewhat, only to be followed by the worse drought of the 1980s.

Even in the relatively good times in 1978, Niger was in the apparently odd position of having too little food to feed its population adequately but being a net *exporter* of food. In fact, as Figure 4.1 shows, this position was shared by more than a dozen other less developed countries, including China and Pakistan, so it is certainly not unusual. The explanation is

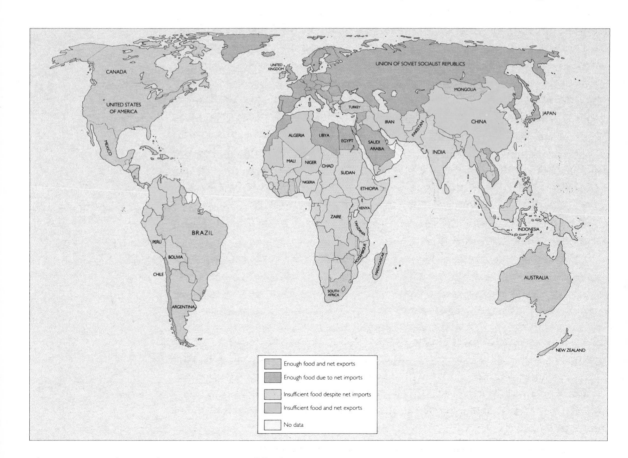

Figure 4.1 *Food imports/exports against overall food requirements.*

simple: about a quarter of the cultivable land in less developed countries is used to grow cash crops for export to the markets of the industrialised world. These crops are economically vital – 60 per cent of Africa's export earnings come from coffee and cocoa and 70 per cent of Latin America's from sugar, coffee and soya beans – but much of the trade is in the hands of multinational corporations, who either organise production on their own plantations, often using machinery and chemicals, or buy from small producers. For most of the post-war period the value of these exports has decreased in relation to the cost of manufactured imports so the net benefit to less developed countries has been limited. In the case of sugar, cane growers have been hard hit by exclusion of their product from the EC (in the face of subsidised beet sugar) and the USA (as food manufacturers substituted subsidised corn syrup for sugar). Nor has the problem of trade been overcome by aid. Even in 1985 when Band Aid stimulated unprecedented donations by charities and governments and a massive £2,500 million went to African countries experiencing or threatened by famine, those same countries paid twice that sum in debt repayments to banks in developed countries. During the 1980s Africa's food production per capita declined by 1.1 per cent per year.

This brief look at the experience of farmers in Niger suggests that they can produce food in extremely difficult environments and are responsive to innovations which increase their income and/or protect the environment. However, their problems have been increased by their incorporation into a global system of food production and trade which sought to expand production in ways which were neither sustainable nor equitable. These new methods are often described as the successful methods used in advanced countries. But it is important to establish exactly what are the criteria by which success is judged. The issues of productivity and sustainability are considered in the next two sections.

Productivity

The commonsense image of agricultural productivity is that rich countries are highly productive and poor countries relatively unproductive. At first sight, the data seem to confirm this: the less developed countries produce half of world agricultural output by value, but have three-quarters of the population and 93 per cent of the agricultural labour force. However, a moment's reflection is enough to put this in doubt:

- 'developed' agriculture uses far more energy, machinery and chemicals, so the *value added* in agriculture is much less

- some developed countries, especially in the EC, subsidise agriculture to produce far more than would otherwise be possible

- rich country consumers can afford to pay higher prices

- figures for the value of less developed country production are probably underestimates because they omit food grown for subsistence

- values are converted into US dollars on the basis of exchange rates which may undervalue less developed country currencies.

It's obvious that there are great difficulties in comparing such different ways of producing food. These are compounded by the fact that the value of agricultural output is only a fraction of that of industrial and service output: one-twentieth in the industrialised world as against one-fifth in less developed countries. They are further compounded by the way that different measures of productivity give different results.

Measures of productivity should relate outputs to inputs. Because agriculture produces such a range of outputs and is mainly for profit rather than subsistence, value is a more useful measure of output than weight or energy content. In principle, the ideal measure should establish the value of all inputs (land, labour, machinery, fuel, chemicals and seed) but even in developed countries this information is not available. What is available for most countries is a measure of value added in agriculture, i.e. the value of outputs less the value of immediate inputs (fuel, seed, fertilisers etc.). The measure of value added can be related to other widely available data on the area of land used for agriculture and on the number of people in the agricultural labour force. The variation in figures for value added per person differ startlingly from those for value added per hectare.

The map (Figure 4.2) of value added per capita contains few surprises. It shows high labour productivity in Europe, the US, Canada, Australia and Argentina. Conversely, labour productivity is low throughout Africa and Asia (except Japan). Latin America is more productive than Asia, but far below the levels of the developed countries. This pattern is consistent with the division shown in Figure 4.1 between countries with sufficient food and those without. It is also consistent with what we know about progressive European agriculture, where efficiency is said to be indicated by increased farm size, mechanisation, use of artificial fertilisers, herbicides and insecticides, together with a dramatic reduction in the agricultural labour force. However, we must remember that this is efficiency measured in use of labour and in economic terms. But even in economic terms, it depends on enormous subsidies both for structural improvements (like improved drainage, hedgerow removal and ploughing of heathland) and to support prices. Even after these subsidies Europe remains dependent on imports to feed both human and animal populations. In the late 1980s, the

Overcrowded, often dependent on imported feed and producing severe problems of slurry disposal, intensive pig farming creates a range of moral and practical problems.

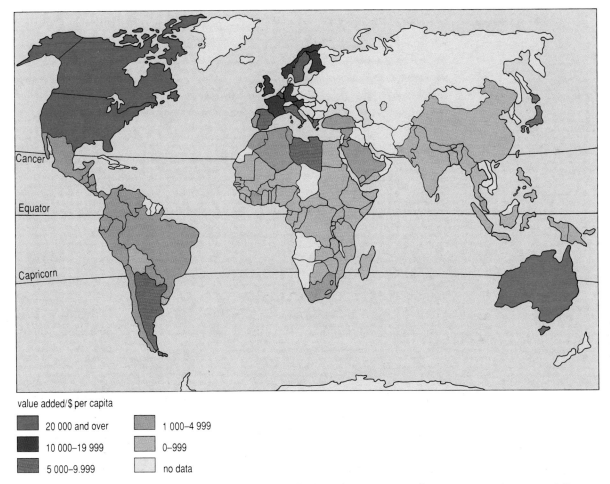

value added/$ per capita

20 000 and over	1 000–4 999
10 000–19 999	0–999
5 000–9.999	no data

Figure 4.2 *Value added in agriculture, 1982 (per capita of the population economically active in agriculture, in US dollars).*

EC imported over five million tonnes of cereals, over 20 million tonnes of cereal substitutes like manioc and nearly 30 million tonnes of protein rich products, especially soya cake, for use as animal feed. This made up 40 per cent of purchased inputs to EC agriculture (as against 12 per cent for fertilisers, 12 per cent for machinery, 10 per cent for fuel and five per cent for other chemicals). A substantial proportion of these imports come from less developed countries and most of it is used for intensive production of livestock in systems like battery chickens, indoor pigs, feed lot beef and zero grazed dairy cows. Not only are these practices increasingly criticised in terms of ethics and of food quality, they are creating some serious environmental impacts because of the volume of wastes that have to be disposed of.

The map (Figure 4.3) of value added per hectare *does* contain some surprises. Western Europe and Japan are in the highest category – but are matched by Egypt, Mauritania and Papua New Guinea. Ethiopia and Sudan are at the low end of the scale – but so are Australia, Argentina and North America, which are all major food exporters. Perhaps most striking is that China matches the UK on this measure and outstrips the USA. So the measure of value added per hectare challenges the common stereotypes of the productivity of different countries and types of agriculture. Some of the surprising results can be explained quite simply. The high figures for Egypt, Mauritania and Papua New Guinea actually relate to small parts of those countries where irrigation is used for intensive commercial production or small areas of plantation are used for export crops. The USA and Australia produce a great deal of wheat from semi-arid areas where yields

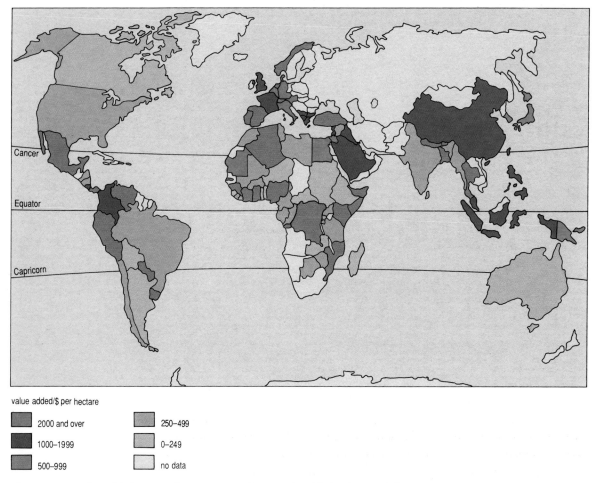

value added/$ per hectare

◼ 2000 and over   ◼ 250–499

◼ 1000–1999   ◻ 0–249

◼ 500–999   ◻ no data

Figure 4.3 *Value added in agriculture, 1982 (per hectare of arable land, in US dollars).*

The cooler climate of the Cameron Highlands, Malaysia offers conditions in which vegetables can be produced by labour intensive methods.

are kept low by lack of water and mechanisation enables one farmer to handle very large areas. But the strong performance of East Asian countries with large populations and high value added per hectare cannot be written off as an aberration. It results from a different approach to intensive production from that of developed 'western' countries.

Whereas agricultural populations in developed countries have declined for many decades, agricultural populations in many less developed countries have continued to grow in spite of increased migration to the cities. In much of Africa and Asia, over 60 per cent of the labour force still works on the land. The result has been a progressive increase in the amount of labour expended on each piece of land, reaching 250 or more person-days per hectare in some cases, notably the wet rice culture which produces nearly half of the cereals grown in less developed countries. In the last 30 years, rice output has more than doubled and in 1985 total cereal output in less developed countries exceeded that in the developed countries for the first time since records began. This so-called Green Revolution saw science applied to intensive rice production.

Paddy rice and the Green Revolution

Wet rice cultivation has a 7,000 year history and now produces about three-quarters of the world's rice, especially in Asia. The rice plant, unlike other cereals, can grow in flooded soils because it has channels which supply air to the roots. Flooded cultivation has significant advantages: it alters soil structure, reducing loss of water and nutrients by percolation, and its chemistry, eliminating extremes of acidity and alkalinity and allowing nutrients to cycle efficiently. Continuous flooding is more efficient in all these respects than intermittent flooding. Building, maintenance and operation of reservoirs and channels demand large inputs of labour and so do processes like transplanting, fertilising with organic waste and simultaneous use for ducks and fish. But these traditional methods have provided rice for subsistence and, from the nineteenth century, allowed expansion of production by the colonial powers in order to feed workers on tea and rubber plantations.

The methods used in rice production have been modernised since the 1920s, often led by the Japanese. Large-scale use of mechanisation was rejected early and advances have included small-scale machinery (especially electric pumps instead of human powered pumps), closer control of water levels, imported fertilisers (at first organic, later chemical) and selective breeding. Between 1900 and 1970 productivity of rice farming in Japan doubled per hectare and quadrupled per capita. However, the system was still very labour intensive, absorbing 1,729 hours of labour per hectare per year, whereas American wheat farmers used just seven hours per hectare!

The early Japanese advances were taken up by the International Rice Research Institute, established in 1960 in the Philippines with funding from the Ford and Rockefeller Foundations. The IRRI has produced a series of high yielding varieties (HYVs) which have taken many Asian countries from food deficit to surplus.

The Green Revolution brought about by the use of HYVs has had some unfortunate side-effects because HYVs had to be used with large inputs of fertiliser, weedkillers and pesticides. Landlords and larger producers were better able to afford those inputs, so they have gained while tenants and small producers have not. The indiscriminate use of chemicals damaged fish and duck output as well as polluting human water supplies. The introduction of new insect resistant varieties and more selective pesticides have made it possible to reduce the use of pesticides. However, the problem of social inequalities has proved harder to solve.

To sum up, this brief look at productivity has shown a sharp discrepancy between systems which seek to minimise labour input and those which seek to maximise output per hectare. In a world with a fixed amount of cultivable land and rapidly growing populations, output per hectare seems likely to be increasingly valued in the future. This leads one to look with some scepticism at developed agriculture and this scepticism can only increase when one considers its long-term sustainability.

Sustainability

In the case of Niger, we saw that maintaining the output of agriculture on a sustainable basis involved conservation of soil and water by enhancing vegetation cover. In developed countries, soil conservation is also a problem, but two other factors also threaten the sustainability of current systems of agriculture: dependence on energy inputs and the public's continued willingness to pay subsidies.

Soil degradation and conservation

Soil forms very slowly so current agriculture depends on soils built up over millennia under natural vegetation, possibly sustained or enhanced by systems of mixed farming using animal manure and vegetable wastes to sustain soil structure and improve the retention of moisture and nutrients. Yet modern farming methods endanger the soil in a number of ways: heavy machinery may compact soil, clearance of vegetation exposes the surface to wind and water, harvesting of crops removes nutrients, irrigation poses the problem of salinisation and overgrazing can strip vegetation cover.

We tend to associate soil degradation with areas like the Sahel, but in fact it is very widespread, affecting one-quarter to one-third of the world's arable lands. The dustbowl of the Great Plains of the United States in the 1930s was an early *cause célèbre*, showing what can happen when topsoil is exposed to drought and wind. Today, a range of conservation practices are used to protect the soil from wind but the Great Plains still experience crop loss and soil erosion on a large scale – affecting nearly a million hectares in 1981 and decimating production in 1988. The United States Department of Agriculture estimate that over one-quarter of US arable land is losing soil at an unsustainable rate.

Erosion by running water is an even more serious problem world-wide and one which is worsened by ploughing steep slopes. In less developed countries, population pressure leads to cultivation of steep slopes and intense rainfall causes gullying. Even in England's South Downs, conversion of grassland to cereal production has led to serious erosion. Larger fields, cultivation of a single crop over wide areas and lack of organic material in the soil all contribute to erosion.

Another serious form of soil degradation is the salinisation that so often occurs in irrigated areas. This has been known for thousands of years in the valleys of the Tigris and Euphrates but is now widespread in the Middle East, India, Pakistan and also in the USA, where about one-third of irrigated land in the south west is affected. The problem arises when excessive amounts of irrigation water and inadequate drainage combine to raise the water table and bring saline groundwater to the surface where it evaporates, leaving a crust of salt. The same process is happening in Western Australia, where some five million hectares are threatened by salinisation brought on by removal of tree cover and where whole river systems are becoming too saline for irrigation or water supply. So, although desertification affects poor countries most severely, it also occurs in some of the world's most affluent countries.

Energy dependence

Modern agriculture is highly dependent on manufactured inputs. Indeed these contribute half of the value of output in many cases. One of the most important inputs, directly as fuel and indirectly in making machinery, fertilisers and chemicals, is energy and especially energy derived from petroleum. In the USA the amount of commercial energy used to produce a given weight of food increased fivefold between 1900 and 1970. Rice production in the USA consumes seven times as much commercial energy per kilo as rice produced in the Philippines. Because developed agriculture produces a higher proportion of animal products, more energy is used to transport animals and feed, to heat and light buildings and to process the products. Feed lot beef is eight times as energy intensive as rice.

At present, with world oil prices relatively low, this energy dependence is not a problem. However the oil crisis of the mid-1970s and the smaller price rise at the time of the Gulf War indicate that the viability of these methods is doubtful even in the short term. In the long term, even the oil companies see supplies becoming scarce by the middle of the next century. Whether or not new sources of energy can be found is a question discussed in Chapter 7, but meanwhile it should not be taken for granted that massive energy inputs can be sustained.

Subsidy, environmental impact and food quality

In 1986 the USA subsidised agriculture by $26 million and the EC by $22 million. Since then these subsidies have been reduced, more rapidly in the USA. Politicians and the public have become more aware that subsidies promote intensification of production in ways which have damaging consequences to the environment, food quality, animal conditions and international trade.

You may already have noted that the 'structural improvements' funded by the EC included many landscape changes criticised by environmentalists: removal of hedges, ploughing of grassland (for example on Exmoor and the chalk Downs), drainage, (whether of small ponds or large areas of wetland, most acrimoniously in the case of the Norfolk Broads grazing marshes), construction of large silos or animal sheds, clearance of broad-leaved woods, and liming and fertilising of upland pasture.

Both increased use of chemicals for crop production and intensive animal rearing have had damaging effects on water quality. Much of this has been local and intermittent, especially where animal slurry enters streams, causes deoxygenation and the death of fish and plants, or where local releases of pesticides exceed the maximum admissible concentrations. Increasingly, however, nitrates are being found in water supplies in much of Eastern England and, though there are disputes as to whether this is a health hazard, many members of the public are demanding controls of fertiliser use and maintenance of higher quality standards for water.

Nitrate and pesticide residues in food products have caused some alarm, but in Britain at least, public alarm about food quality has focused on animal products. In 1989–90, an increase in food poisoning led to the revelation that salmonella bacteria were not only endemic in most commercial chicken flocks but also beginning to affect eggs for the first time. Simultaneously, the new cattle disease BSE was shown to result from cattle feed containing the offal of sheep infected with scrapie. The unprecedented transfer of a disease from one species to another led to fears that transfer to humans might be possible. The incorporation of animal offal in cattle feed also drew attention to the intensive regimes now being used and led more people to question the ethics of subjecting animals to these crowded and artificial conditions.

The wide range of problems affecting the agriculture of developed countries has led to a search for policy solutions. It has been widely agreed that surpluses, environmental impacts and food quality problems could be tackled by a policy of *extensification* – reducing inputs like fertilisers and pesticides. The EC has responded with the policy of 'set aside', where farmers are paid to take a fraction of their land out of production. However, this leaves them free to intensify further their management of the remaining land, so energy and chemical inputs are likely to increase. Only in a minority of Environmentally Sensitive Areas has the EC been willing to move towards subsidy of environmentally friendly practices, including extensification.

▷ *Use of clover to fix nitrogen and the presence of some weeds are indicators of methods which avoid reliance on chemical fertilisers, weedkillers and pesticides.*

The willingness of the EC to cut farm subsidies had a major impact on the whole of world trade as it led to the breakdown early in 1991 of the so-called Uruguay round of the General Agreement on Tariffs and Trade (GATT) – the rules which regulate world trade in every kind of product. The EC was under severe pressure from the USA, Australia and New Zealand (all, as we have seen, major food exporters) to lower subsidies dramatically and allow a free market in food. This would remove some of the distortions of current trade relations, but other provisions seemed calculated to weaken both environmental protection and less developed economies. Negotiations over GATT are bound to be reopened sooner or later and it is to be hoped that they may be influenced by the spirit of the Brandt and Brundtland Reports rather than by the short-term self-interest of the most affluent industrialised countries.

Conclusion

This chapter has argued that the very real agricultural problems of countries like Niger are compounded by the way the current system of world trade works. Developed agriculture, and especially that of the EC, makes demands on the less developed countries for animal feed and impacts upon it by dumping surplus produce, both of which damage its ability to feed itself. Many less developed countries have shown their resilience, especially in the 1960s through the Green Revolution, though progress was much slower from the 1970s, especially in Africa. Even the apparently successful developed country agriculture is economically unsound, environmentally damaging and doubtful in sustainability. Developed countries need to change as much as do the less developed – indeed more, since they dominate world trade.

A revised policy should both reduce environmental impacts in the rich countries and enhance poor producers' ability to sell their produce. A policy which would benefit both would be to raise the price and lower the volume of imported animal feed: this would reduce the environmental impacts of intensive livestock production in the developed countries and increase food availability and incomes in less developed countries. Similarly a policy of extensification of industrialised agriculture would release supplies of fertilisers and chemicals which could be offered to poor producers at a subsidised rate, using funds saved by not subsidising so-called 'structural improvements' in the developed countries.

However, many barriers remain before an environmentally sound and secure system of food production can be achieved. Governments persist in pursuing narrow self-interest: witness the spending of 60 per cent of EC budgets on subsidies to European farmers and one per cent on aid to less developed countries. Also, many countries have inequitable systems of landholding and agricultural systems in thrall to urban consumers and/or industrial interests. Chapter 9 discusses the way these problems of agriculture and environment are being addressed in the international debates stimulated by the Brundtland report.

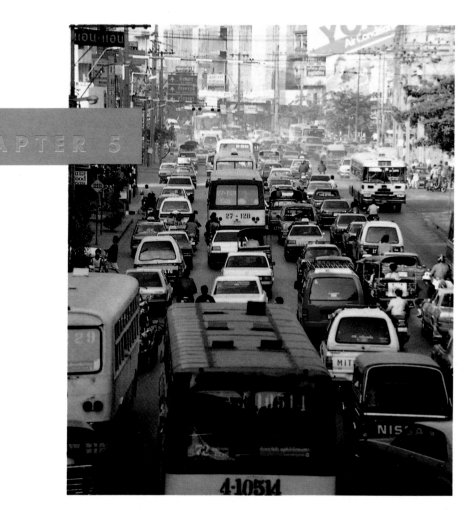

CHAPTER 5

Urban crisis

'Up until recently the people living in Bangkok had to pay more attention to raising their own standard of living. It's only recently that the people have been able to pay more attention to environmental matters. Without public pressure then politicians and decision-makers will not give the environment its new priority. That is why not enough financial resources have been allocated to solving the problems.'

Dr Dhira Phantumvanit, December 1989.

In 1950 about 750 million people, a little over one-quarter of the world's total population at that time, lived in urban centres. By the turn of the century, according to recent United Nations' estimates, almost half of humanity, a projected 2.8 billion people, will be 'urbanised'; 75 per cent of this growth will have taken place in the less developed world. Table 5.1 gives a global breakdown of the figures, both actual and estimated.

Table 5.1 Population living in urban areas, 1950 – 2000 (projected)

	1950	1985	2000
	per cent		
World total	29.2	41.0	46.6
Developed regions	53.8	71.5	74.4
Developing regions	17.0	31.2	39.3
	millions		
World total	734.2	1,982.8	2,853.6
Developed regions	447.3	838.8	949.9
Developing regions	286.8	1,144.0	1,903.7

UNCED (1987) *Our Common Future* (the Brundtland Report), Chapter 9, p. 236.

Growth of this magnitude is already putting the severest pressure on the governments of the developing countries to produce and manage urban infrastructures, services and shelter. For although the rate of population growth in the less developed countries is beginning to slow down, the major increases in the 1990s and beyond will continue to be in cities in the less developed world. Of course, the industrialised nations have their urban problems, but here, arguably, it is ultimately a matter for political expediency and social choice. For the less developed world it is a matter of urban crisis, though this is not to deny the existence of certain elements of political and social choice here also.

This chapter examines some of the principal environmental problems confronting cities in the less developed world in order to gain an understanding of the relationship between rapid urban development and environmental impact, and evaluates the type of policy responses being put

◁ *Previous page*
Traffic congestion in central Bangkok.

forward to tackle these problems. The justification for undertaking this analysis in a developing world context is that specific attention is focused on the connections between such problems and economic development.

A case study of Bangkok, the capital of Thailand, illustrates how a combination of urban problems, associated on the one hand with disadvantage, low income and poverty, and on the other hand with rapid development, has produced growth of a particular form with particular damaging effects. We will then assess how far this example is representative of urban development problems globally and draw some comparisons with Mexico City, currently the most populated urban area in the world. An analysis of causes emphasises both the *environmental effects* of growth and the *social processes* involved. In a real sense development may be seen to be aggravating environmental problems which are already serious and we challenge the argument that economic development *per se* can be a sufficient solution to urban problems.

A development problem?

The expansion of the major cities of the developing world has been as alarming as it has been remarkable. The population of Mexico City rose from three million in 1950 to over 16 million in the early 1980s, and UN forecasts project a figure in excess of 25 million by the year 2000. The same forecasts see the population of Sao Paulo in Brazil almost doubling from 12.5 million in 1980 to 24 million by 2000.

The rate of growth in Bangkok has been no less dramatic. From a modest city of some half million people in 1950, it had expanded by 1990 to over eight million, including an estimated 1.5 million unregistered immigrants, making it the fourteenth largest city in the world. This increase has been accompanied by, and indeed has been directly related to, a prolonged period of sustained economic development. Between 1960 and 1990 the Thai economy grew at an average annual rate of 7.5 per cent, and in the early 1990s the prediction was for an expansion of up to 10 per cent per annum, with indicators suggesting continued high growth in virtually every sector of the economy. Such economic growth puts Thailand amongst the *Asian Tigers* of industrialisation, alongside South Korea, Singapore and Taiwan; but unlike these nations Thailand still maintains its developing country status, the majority of the population still being employed in primary production, mainly agriculture, and living in rural areas.

The paradox is that such economic dynamism co-exists with severe social and environmental problems, which are brought into sharpest focus in the capital city itself. As Dr Dhira Phantumvanit, Director of the Thailand Development Research Unit explains:

> 'I would say that our environmental issues are not unlike those in other big cities of the Third World. What happened first of all is that there has been a tremendous amount of population pressure. One has to be reminded that in the Third World there is this big discrepancy between rural and urban areas. That is why there is always this forced migration to big cities and that is the root of the problem – of the environmental problems. Now when you couple that with economic growth and industrialisation, what happens is that investment in pollution control infrastructure is left behind. We do not have proper sewage treatment systems.'

Recorded interview, Bangkok, December 1989.

The growth of population has already far exceeded the rate of growth of formal economic opportunities and many of Bangkok's inhabitants survive on very low incomes. Urban poverty is indeed an acute problem in all the major cities of the developing world and Bangkok is no exception.

Placed in the context of a burgeoning economy and a great deal of wealth unevenly distributed, there are many people in Bangkok whose bargaining position is very weak, particularly when it comes to access to land. The urban poor represent a significant *underclass* who are condemned to eke out an existence in the marginal areas of the city where there are risks from flooding, air and water pollution, and the disposal of rubbish and waste. Presently, only two per cent of Bangkok's population is connected to the city's sewer network. Most raw sewage goes directly into the *klongs* (canals), the living environment for many of the poor.

Ultra-modern architecture in the heart of Bangkok's Central Business District.

A typical slum dwelling on the side of a klong close to the centre of Bangkok.

An environment problem?

Bangkok raises a series of questions, not only about the overall effects of rapid economic growth, but also about the differential impact of development on people's living environments. There is a growing awareness of the environmental problems that exist in the cities of the less developed world generally. The information in the box, an extract from the UN World Commission on Environment and Development Report, is typical of the way in which the 'facts' are presented to us.

Environmental problems in cities of the less developed world

'Out of India's 3,119 towns and cities, only 209 had partial and only eight had full sewage and sewage treatment facilities. On the river Ganges, 114 cities, each with 50,000 or more inhabitants, dump untreated sewage into the river each day. DDT factories, tanneries, paper and pulp mills, petrochemical and fertiliser complexes, rubber factories, and a host of others use the river to get rid of their wastes.

'Chinese industries are concentrated around 20 cities and ensure a high level of air pollution. Lung cancer mortality in Chinese cities is four to seven times higher than in the nation as a whole, and the difference is largely attributable to heavy air pollution.

'In Malaysia, the highly urbanised Klang Valley has two to three times the pollution levels of major cities in the United States, and the Klang river system is heavily contaminated with agricultural and industrial effluents and sewage.'

UNCED Report Our Common Future, *1987.*

To what extent are the problems described in the box purely *physical,* to which there are technical solutions, and to what extent are they social, economic and political? If the *causes* of the problems are related to economic and industrial development, then how can development also provide the *solutions*? This seeming contradiction can be explored further in the case of Bangkok.

Bangkok: an environment and development problem

Bangkok, located on the Chao Phrya river, has always provided a focus for economic activity. As industrialisation has continued apace, the economic relations of the country have become progressively oriented towards the city, to the extent that, for instance, over 75 per cent of Thailand's factories dealing with hazardous chemicals are now located within Bangkok's hinterland. The growth of private transport has been equally phenomenal and the city is fast becoming choked with traffic. It has reputedly been calculated that the average speed of travel during the 'rush hour' is two miles per hour and the rush hour lasts all day!

If one had to underline the most fundamental feature of environmental deterioration resulting from a combination of rapid industrialisation and population growth in the cities of the less developed world, then it would surely have to be the supply and quality of water. Bangkok's remarkable growth, allied to the city's geographical location, has presented the Metropolitan Authority with the severest of managerial challenges, not just in technical terms but politically and economically also.

The principal problems are interlinked: insufficient water supply, water pollution from domestic and industrial waste, flooding and land subsidence. Because growing demand is increasingly outstripping the Authority's ability to supply adequate water of satisfactory quality, the city's underground aquifers are being over-pumped to the extent that the land surface is subsiding by as much as 100 mm per year in some places. In 1990 an estimated one-third of water abstracted was unlicensed and therefore illegal. At this rate, without further political intervention, Bangkok could be literally under water by 2005. (The city is currently an average of 1.5 metres above mean sea level and this estimation takes no account of the possible effects of global warming.)

The combination of a sinking city, heavy monsoon rains and the removal of large areas of forest cover in northern Thailand has resulted in frequent and increasingly damaging floods. Following public outrage over floods and landslides in southern Thailand (including Bangkok) which caused widespread death and destruction in 1988, the Thai Government imposed a nationwide ban on logging in January 1989. Nevertheless, such belated action has done little to resolve the problem and there is still social unease, even though the people most affected (those living in the most vulnerable locations on the banks of the rivers and the klongs) are those with the least effective political voice, the urban poor.

Frequent flooding exacerbates the already serious problem of water pollution. There is no effective overall sewerage treatment system, a lack

The aftermath of floods and mud slides in Katoon, Thailand, following the monsoon rains of 1988.

of facilities to deal with waste disposal generally, and what regulations do exist to control the worst excesses of dumping industrial effluent and so on are poorly enforced. Much needed research into levels of pollution is beginning to provide the sort of information required as a basis for action, but a number of question marks remain concerning the degree of political will and the finance available to develop an infrastructure capable of coping with an increasingly critical situation.

Tackling the problem

Living in Bangkok is becoming more and more hazardous. Such is the city's legacy from four decades of uncontrolled and largely unplanned growth, and as population, industry and transport continue to grow, the dilemma for the politicians heightens. It is certainly the case, as it is in all developing cities, that the urban underclasses are suffering the most and carry the

For millions of Bangkok's citizens the klongs (canals) are their main source of water for washing and drinking.

least political clout, but the problems are beginning to affect everyone. Here is an extract from a letter from one concerned citizen:

> 'It seems not enough to learn from other countries' experiences; we have to be a Newly Industrialised Country (NIC) and learn the lesson first hand. Unfortunately, by the time we learn being an NIC is not to the advantage of Thailand, which is basically an agricultural country, it will be too late. Once fertile farmlands have been turned into factory sites, beaches and forest reserves have become tourist resorts, paralysed traffic has become a way of life, the air has become heavy with industrial smoke in Bangkok, and there will be more natural disasters to contend with as Nature takes her revenge on us.'
>
> Bangkok Post, *26 November 1989.*

Such expressions of *middle class* anxiety find many an echo in the industrialised world, where the growth of campaigning pressure groups has been one of the hallmarks of the 'environmental movement' for 20 years or more. Their emergence in the less developed world certainly reflects a similar awareness, but underlying it there is also a sense of 'We don't want to make the same mistakes as you have, but it looks as though we are … isn't there another way?' Groups like Magic Eyes in Bangkok, campaigning against the indiscriminate dumping of rubbish and for cleaning up the Chao Phrya river, are seeking tighter controls and more effective environmental legislation.

Central to a consideration of 'tackling the problem' is the way in which the relationship between environment and development is perceived – by the various actors in Bangkok (politicians, government agencies, industrialists, pressure groups, ordinary people) and by us in the more developed world. There are a number of strands of thought that need unravelling here. Thailand is rapidly becoming more industrial and in so doing is increasing its per capita GNP in relation to other countries in the 'Asian league'. It is striving for growth in order to develop its way out of poverty and, because it is a structurally stable nation in a South East Asian context, it is an attractive proposition for Western investment and multinational expansion.

How far can this be seen in terms of 'inevitable trap' or 'ultimate salvation'? Capitalist industrial development brings its rewards in terms of improving everyone's lot, even if this does happen on an inequitable basis, but there is a price to be paid environmentally. Then again, if the more developed nations are beginning to get the balance right between environment and development (and this is quite a big 'if' as Chapters 9 and 10 contest), is this not the most hopeful path for the less developed nations to tread also? Optimistically, we could argue in the UK that our cities are far healthier places than they were when Charles Dickens was providing graphic descriptions of squalor and deprivation, so things should improve in cities like Bangkok, although there is much less time available.

Gro Harlem Brundtland puts it this way: 'It is both futile and indeed an insult to the poor to tell them that they must remain in poverty to protect the environment'. This is effectively in answer to those who live exclusively in the more developed world and would see environmental protection at the top of any political agenda without reservation.

A political dilemma?

Do the political leaders in Thailand, and particularly in Bangkok, have *any* choices? Compared with say India, which has only one-third the per capita GNP, there would certainly appear to be economic scope for improvement. The technology and the knowhow exist, both within the country and in the form of international co-operation and technology transfer, to deal with the major infrastructural problems confronting the city: setting up a network of water treatment plants, comprehensive flood protection schemes, a centralised sewerage treatment system, a programme for recharging the underground aquifers, and an efficient public transport system.

Some senior political and economic advisers express a guarded optimism that real progress towards *sustainable development* is being made in Bangkok. Environmental legislation, in the form of pricing policies for water and for safeguarding against the worst effects of pollution on the 'polluter pays' principle, is being debated; but a proposed water rating system is already meeting strong resistance, especially from the private sector.

▶ *A heavily polluted river in Bangkok.*

Even if the political will does exist to tackle the most serious environmental and social issues, the principal constraints are likely to remain economic ones. The problem with large-scale solutions favoured by governments and international agencies is the huge costs involved which are not easily recoverable. Cheaper small-scale schemes may have some local benefits, but are unlikely to be sufficient to tackle the longer-term problems; and the tendency is for governments to think only in the short term.

Lessons from the more developed world tell us that we can only expect so much from governments anyway. Leaders of social justice movements in Bangkok, like Asian Housing Rights, argue that it is the private sector and not the Government that really holds the key to the environmental future of the city. Raising public awareness and increasing public pressure are important features of the modern industrial state.

However, few involved in grassroots movements in Bangkok are optimistic about the Government's ability or even willingness to woo big business to enter into a partnership to safeguard the environment. That would be a pretty radical agenda for any nation, developed or otherwise. Somsook Boonybancha of Asian Housing Rights sums it up thus:

'In the past five years the society is growing so fast that now the predominant policy is to privatise all kinds of development. So the growing group in the society now is the private investor. But the people in the communities are still looking to the Government as the target, but I would say that the Government is not so strong. They are also trying to privatise development. So when you ask which group the people of Thailand should target, I would say we are in a very confusing stage at the moment.'

Recorded interview, Bangkok, November 1989.

A broader view: crisis or challenge?

By focusing thus far on Bangkok the chapter has refrained from taking an overly pessimistic view of urban environmental problems in developing countries. Whilst the city's problems are undoubtedly very serious and it would be quite justifiable to talk in terms of a 'crisis', it would be equally valid to speak about the challenge facing Thailand's leaders (political, economic, industrial and social), and the people themselves. Whilst issues of equity and social justice are never far from the surface, especially amongst the social activists who represent some of the inhabitants of the worst slums under the urban motorways, there is a general sense of achievement, progress and urgency to improve things in the city as a whole.

That may in part be a subjective interpretation, but it is also recognition of Thailand's attempts to confront the problems and to limit, as far as possible, the concentration of growth in Bangkok and the surrounding region and to channel development to other areas. Economic growth may have its harmful and unpleasant side-effects but if abject poverty is the alternative then that isn't much of a choice. This case was effectively put at a UNCED public hearing in Sao Paulo, Brazil, in 1985:

'The shanty towns have found their own resources without any assistance from anyone else. The real problem is not that. It is the poverty, the lack of planning, the lack of technical assistance, the lack of financing to buy materials, the lack of urban equipment … Generally speaking, it seems clear that without meeting the basic needs of human beings, concern for the environment has to be secondary. Man has to survive, answer and attend first to his basic survival needs – food, housing, sanitation – and then to the environment.'

Walter Pinto Costa, Sao Paulo, 28–29 October 1985.

▲ *Shanty town developments in Mexico City.*

In the league table of the cities of less developed countries, an assessment based on the criteria of growth and prosperity would have Bangkok as being relatively well off. It has the problems but not on the scale or of the order of say Mexico City, Sao Paulo or Calcutta. In most cities in the less developed world the ever increasing pressure for shelter and basic services has taken its toll on the urban fabric. The essential infrastructure – water supply, roads, public transport, waste disposal services – is very often in a state of disrepair and decay. Certain diseases (dysentery, typhoid, hepatitis) have become endemic in the slum areas. Because of the concentration of industry in urban areas, with the minimum of controls and outmoded (by Western standards) technology, air pollution has become a very serious issue, a point already noted in Bangkok and in the box on page 78. Table 5.2 provides some comparative figures for more and less developed countries.

Table 5.2 Air pollution levels in selected cities, 1982 –1985

	Peak levels of particulate matter	Peak levels of sulphur dioxide
		(Microgrammes per cubic metre)
More developed countries		
Brussels (Belgium)	97	205
Copenhagen (Denmark)	383	135
Frankfurt (Germany)	117	230
London (UK)	77	171
New York City (USA)	121	131
Warsaw (Poland)	248	205
Less developed countries		
Bangkok (Thailand)	741	48
Beijing (China)	1307	625
Calcutta (India)	967	188
Delhi (India)	1062	197
Manila (Philippines)	579	198
Sao Paulo (Brazil)	338	173

World Resources Institute, 1988

What causes a poor urban environment?

The previous paragraph has underlined the most significant features of what makes for a poor urban environment. Taking a broad perspective within the less developed world generally, it sounds very much like a crisis situation. We can clearly see the environmental effects but what are the basic causes of urban degradation and social deprivation? There are plenty of clues in the foregoing text. Essentially, it comes back to the relationship between environment and development. On the one hand, economic and technological development do offer the potential and the prospect of 'cures' for problems of housing, services and pollution – it can certainly be argued that higher living standards do allow for the provision of better buildings, piped water and sewage treatment. Yet on the other hand, as we have seen in Bangkok, these also cause some of the worst problems, from air and water pollution to waste disposal and congestion. Development is a value-laden term and is really too general to be helpful. What matters is the form of development.

The most basic problem in the developing cities is that of income generation, which is inextricably linked to the issues of poverty and inequity. The lack of sufficient well paid, safe and rewarding work is widely regarded as the most significant contributory factor to the poor urban environment. Clearly, conditions vary a great deal from city to city, but generally the majority of workers are engaged in low productivity work, often in very dangerous environments. Even where cities have succeeded in developing major industrial sectors, economic development has rarely kept pace with population growth (both from natural increase and immigration), as is the case in Bangkok.

In the absence of any state financed social security or benefit system, many inhabitants are obliged to obtain some form of livelihood in what is termed the *informal economy* , in order to survive from one day to the next. Activities can range from street vending to raking through rubbish tips. In fact, it is not easy to be unemployed in a developing city. Often workers with secondary school education are more likely to be unemployed than those with less education.

Consequently, the rates of recorded unemployment in developing cities are much lower than we might expect. Indeed many cities in the UK had higher recorded unemployment rates during the 1980s than did cities in Latin America, for instance.

The overall effects of poor working conditions on social welfare are obvious. Low wages have knock-on effects and the work situation is undoubtedly at the core of most problems in urban environments in the less developed world. There is a direct correlation between the general poverty of urban societies and the poor quality of their physical environments, and it is not only the level of income that is significant, but also how it is distributed. Look at these examples:

- Manila (1975) the top 10 per cent of income earners received 22 times the average income of the poorest 10 per cent.

- Bogota (1978) the top five per cent of income earners received 25 times the average income of the poorest 20 per cent.

- Bangkok (1985) the top five per cent of income earners received more than 10 times the average income of the poorest 50 per cent.

Unequal distribution of income fosters social segregation: in most developing cities there are very obvious divisions between rich and poor areas. This leads to the creation of a poor social environment in low income neighbourhoods. Prevalence of low incomes means that for the majority of cities the urban tax base is low also, local politics are likely to be unstable and as a result the standard of local government and urban management is poor. All appears to run in a vicious circle, the structural outcome of poverty.

Mexico City: a suitable case for treatment?

Of all the major cities in the less developed world, Mexico City must surely face the greatest environmental and social problems. If, in Bangkok, we saw the adverse consequences of rapid growth and development in a country with a continuously high rate of economic growth, in Mexico City we see the impact of a rapidly rising population – a combination of high natural increase and continuing migration from rural areas – in what is still a relatively poor country.

The current (in 1991) population of over 19 million is expected to rise to 25 million by 2000 according to UN predictions, even though the pace of demographic growth is slowing a little. To many who live in the city, and to many more outside observers, the problems being faced appear insurmountable. If Bangkok's low-lying geographical location is giving cause for

◀ *Part of the urban sprawl that is Mexico City.*

concern, then Mexico City's inhabitants have to contend with living in an earthquake prone area. Records indicate that the city has been struck 122 times since 1460 and the latest serious tremor in 1985 caused widespread death and destruction. Estimates of the total number of fatalities have varied from 10,000 to as many as 60,000. In addition, over 45,000 homes were destroyed or severely damaged, schools catering for 40,000 pupils devastated, and an estimated 40 per cent of the city's hospital beds put out of action.

Still on the natural side, floods are a recurrent threat, as in Bangkok; but it is on the human side, in the social, economic, political and technical processes that contribute to 'urbanisation', that Mexico City attracts the greatest attention as an 'urban nightmare'. Environmental disaster may be waiting in the wings in Bangkok but it has already assumed centre stage in Mexico City.

To describe the symptoms of social deprivation and environmental degradation in Mexico City is to provide a catalogue of some of the worst ills of the developing city: housing conditions are poor – 40 per cent of families live at densities of more than two people per room and 25 per cent live in a 'house' with only one room; sanitation is sub-standard and garbage disposal deficient, both posing major health and pollution problems; road traffic – there are now over 2.75 million vehicles in the city – is causing very serious congestion and air pollution, with smogs a frequent occurrence during the dry half of the year; Mexico City's industrial concentration of oil refineries, power stations and cement works adds to the pollution and to environmental hazards generally; service provision is inadequate, although most homes are supplied with drinking water by one means or another.

▷ *A major source of urban pollution in Mexico City.*

The task facing the city's urban managers is formidable and perhaps not surprisingly much criticism is focused on Government for incompetence and corruption (not unfamiliar accusatory epithets to be levelled at politicians and administrators in the less developed world, or in the more developed world for that matter). Some observers contend that in the circumstances, with more than five million being added to the city's population between 1980 and 1990, the local authorities and government agencies have accomplished a great deal in terms of providing more homes with piped water and mains drainage, improving public transport and building new roads. It can be argued that London has enough problems coping with a population that is actually declining, so perhaps commentators from the more developed world should refrain from being overly critical.

Nevertheless, the crucial problems of ensuring continuous supplies of safe water and progressively reducing air pollution remain unresolved and are indeed bordering on the insoluble. Even an efficient city administration, able to lay its hands on the requisite funds, would have its work cut out to clean up the polluted skies. For here we encounter an all too familiar story, to be taken up in Chapter 8 on global warming: that of political conflict surrounding the control of pollution.

There are two principal sources of air pollution: motor vehicles and heavy industry. Attempts to control the pollution caused by vehicles would be vigorously opposed by the motor industry and indeed by those in government concerned with stimulating economic growth. For it has been the rapid growth of the motor vehicle industry during the past two decades that has contributed significantly to increasing Mexico's GNP. Efforts to impose controls on the major industrial polluters that now contribute around 30 per cent of the total air pollution will also be bitterly contested. If legislation is introduced on the 'polluter pays' principle and production costs rise (as they inevitably would), these will be passed on to the consumer and inflation will rise. Since Mexico experienced very serious inflation during the 1980s, with a rate of 159 per cent in 1987, the last thing the Government wants is further inflationary pressure.

Squaring the circle

This line of argument takes us back to the statement in the introduction that 'in a real sense development may be seen to be aggravating environmental problems which are already serious'. So can 'development', seen solely in terms of *economic development*, be a sufficient solution to urban environmental problems in the less developed world? Or, to put it more simply, can other ways of development be found that do not create so many environmental problems?

Poor urban conditions are the outcome of an unequal world, reflecting the poverty that is endemic in many of the less developed countries. Rural poverty translates into urban poverty, as migrants continue to move into the cities, perceiving conditions to be even worse in the countryside. A shortage of well paid jobs is symptomatic of urban poverty, which in turn leads to poor housing, deficient services, pollution and a degraded environment.

As we have identified in different ways in Bangkok and Mexico City, economic growth is taken to be the only means of breaking the circle of poverty, increasing manufacturing output and generating the wealth which will eventually lead to a better quality of life for everyone – or so the theory goes. Does it have to be the case that there must always be an environmental price to pay as the cost for 'development'?

We enlarge upon this quite fundamental question in Chapters 9 and 10. Clearly, the form that development takes is crucial. It is possible to put forward a 'check-list' of recommendations for the improvement of urban environments generally, involving political, economic, social and technical considerations. The box below provides such a list. There is no simple, straightforward way to improve the urban environment. The industrially advanced nations would be struggling to meet the requirements in the list, let alone less developed countries. Points 1–5 are all technically feasible, given sufficient resources and the political will. Such an intangible concept as 'political will' relates particularly to points 6 –10. Poor countries do not have a great deal of money to spend on improvements even if they choose to so do. For the richer nations the elements of political and social choice are of greater relevance, but the 'urban environmental condition' in many more developed cities leaves a lot to be desired.

It is not at all easy to slow the pace of urban growth nor to reduce the rate of metropolitan expansion, as the examples of Bangkok and Mexico City have demonstrated. One looks for optimistic signs. A good number of northern cities have succeeded in cleaning up their acts, although most still contain pockets of urban deprivation. There are a few other cities, particularly in the Far East (although Bangkok is not yet one of them) that are beginning to come to terms with the relationship between environment and development. In the wider context of the developing world, however, all the signs are that conditions will deteriorate further before they get better, and that is not to be overly pessimistic. Much has to be achieved before conditions can improve.

Check-list for urban improvement

1 The provision of an adequate infrastructure, both large and small scale.

2 The relocation and decentralisation of industry and urban functions.

3 The passing of stricter and more comprehensive legislation and more effective enforcement.

4 The improvement of service facilities for waste disposal, sewage treatment and so on.

5 Better planning of projections for population and economic growth and physical expansion.

6 Attitudinal changes towards environmentally damaging actions.

7 Popular support, the participation of people and pressure on environmental issues.

8 Political will incorporating governmental co-operation and flexibility in political structures.

9 The need to change priorities: not environmental protection versus economic growth, but environment and development aims coinciding.

10 International agreement on the principal objectives of sustainable development.

It may appear to be rather too academic an argument, but if we really want some positive signs we have to look to points 6–10 in the check-list, however long term they may seem, and the more developed world has to face up to its responsibilities in relation to the pace of change, patterns and processes of production and consumption habits. It also has to take a far greater share of the responsibilities facing the less developed world.

We must seriously consider the idea that the only long-term method of improving urban environments in the less developed world is to rethink the whole nature of technological and economic development that has dominated global political and economic processes since the Industrial Revolution, so that it provides better living standards without adverse environmental impacts. At the same time, we need to recognise, as in the case of Bangkok, that at least some of the answer lies outside the city, in rural regeneration programmes, for instance. The nature of change in the countryside itself and the interrelatedness of town and country are significant factors which should not be overlooked.

CHAPTER 6

Minerals: supplies, impacts and regulation

'I think we should learn the fact that – the phrase that's being used so much now is sustainable development – that you can have industry and you can have environment at the same time. While it's not easy I think Sudbury has demonstrated that and is continuing to demonstrate with further emission reductions that such things are possible. It's important to push technology – technology got us into these problems and it's not at all unreasonable to think that technology can get us out of it.'

Tom Brydges, Environment Canada.

Modern society is highly dependent on minerals, whether in raw or refined form. All these materials have to be found, extracted and processed before use and disposed of afterwards. During their 'life cycle' they have a variety of impacts on the environment, ranging from the noise and dust arising from gravel extraction through to potentially lethal effects of toxic or radioactive metals.

To understand the role of minerals in modern society, their impacts on the environment and their likely future availability, this chapter will look briefly at the constituents of the earth's crust, at how economically viable deposits have originated, where they are and how this has affected trade in minerals. The central part of the chapter assesses the impacts of extraction, processing and disposal of minerals, showing that they range from very local to transnational. Finally, we consider methods which have been used in the past to reduce the environmental impacts of mining and industry and look at some proposals for the future. But first, to get a clearer view of the problems, we look at a case study – nickel extraction in Sudbury.

Sudbury: the largest single source of pollution in North America

A classic example of the impacts of mineral extraction is the Sudbury area of Ontario, Canada. This area is the world's main source of nickel, a metal used principally in special steels. The nickel occurs as the sulphide and is mixed with iron and copper sulphides.

Nickel ore is mined both underground and by open-pit methods. Open pit mining may produce 10 or more times as much material per person-shift and is more suited to the very lean grades of ore worked for metals like nickel, copper, lead and zinc. However, it is much more disruptive, producing very large voids and very large amounts of spoil and waste rock.

The nickel ore is crushed and milled down to the size of course sand. The nickel sulphide is separated from the rest of this material by flotation in a column of water pumped upwards and laced with additives like detergents. The waste material, which may be many thousand tonnes per day, is then dumped in tailings ponds which may be hundreds or even thousands of hectares in extent.

The nickel sulphide itself goes to the smelter, where heat and air are used to transform it first to nickel oxide and then, with additional coke, to nickel metal. The necessary removal of the sulphur produces sulphur dioxide gas, one of the major causes of acid rain.

◁ *Previous page*
Mechanised strip mining for coal, Ruhr, Germany.

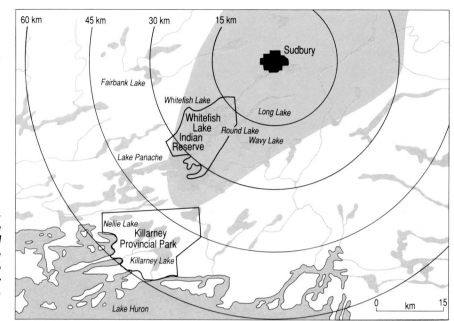

Figure 6.1 *Nickel emissions after the construction of the superstack at Sudbury. Natural lake waters average 10 µg/l while lakes in the shaded area can reach 300 µg/l.*

Lakes of Killarney, Ontario, Canada. The granite bedrock and thin soils made these lakes vulnerable to acidification by sulphur dioxide emitted from Sudbury.

Rehabilitation of land near Sudbury. Casual workers spreading lime as a prelude to seeding to re-establish vegetation cover.

In the early years of mining around Sudbury, the transformation to nickel oxide was achieved by burning huge piles of ore with locally cut timber. The sulphur dioxide was released at ground level and killed vegetation for miles around, producing a landscape which still looks like the surface of the moon. Later, chimneys have been used, culminating in the 387 metre superstack built in 1972 by INCO, one of two multinationals which dominate the supply of nickel. These chimneys have reduced local damage, but only by spreading it over a wider area.

In the 1970s damage was identified as far as 60 km from the smelter. This included raised levels of nickel and copper, caused by emission of very fine particles from the chimney, and acidified lakes and streams. Some lakes, especially on granite bedrock, had pH down to about 4, far too acid for fish to live. The recreational fishery of the Lakes of Killarney provincial park, worth well over a thousand million dollars in 1980, was suffering serious damage.

As the largest single source of pollution in North America, Sudbury has not escaped the attentions of the regulators, indeed the progressive increase of the height of the chimneys was a response to early pressure. The Ontario Ministry of the Environment has been active in two respects; reducing sulphur dioxide emissions and remedial treatment to lakes. The addition of powdered lime did have some beneficial effects, but reductions in acidity were limited and reversible. Reduction at source has been more effective and INCO has made major investments to improve process technology to reduce sulphur dioxide. Levels are well below half of those of the 1970s, with a daily limit of 2,500 tonnes from 1980 and stepped reductions planned down to 265,000 tonnes a year by 1994 – 60 per cent below 1980 levels. The acidity of some lakes which were never limed is now significantly reduced.

Although Sudbury is a special case, it illustrates some of the typical problems of mineral extraction – from voids, through waste rock, acidification of air and water to release of toxic metals. These problems, and ways of reducing them, are considered in a later section. First, however, it is necessary to get a clearer idea of how abundant different minerals are and how this relates to the demand for them.

Minerals in nature and in trade

The major source of all minerals is the rocks of the earth's crust. The minerals of the mantle and the core, however desirable they may be, are totally inaccessible for commercial purposes. Three aspects of minerals are relevant in relation to their use in building or industry: their overall abundance or rarity, the ways they may be locally concentrated and the ease or difficulty of obtaining useful materials, particularly pure elements, from their natural sources. The latter is bound to be a serious problem because earth minerals will mostly be in a chemically stable form and only a handful of elements, for example copper and gold, are stable in their pure forms. Because of this, finding usable deposits of many minerals has been called a geochemical lottery.

Some soluble minerals, such as potash, common salt and gypsum, are left by evaporation of inland seas. The Dead Sea is buoyant because of the high level of dissolved salts.

Abundance

Although around ninety chemical elements occur naturally in the Earth's crust, they vary enormously in their abundance. Two elements are vastly more abundant than any others: oxygen (nearly 47 per cent) and silicon (nearly 28 per cent). Aluminium (eight per cent) and iron (five per cent) follow, then four light metals – calcium, sodium, potassium and magnesium (each two or three per cent). These eight elements make up almost 99 per cent of the crust, so all other elements are relatively rare. Indeed, some commonly used elements such as zinc, copper, nickel and lead occur as only a few dozen parts per million, tin and uranium at two parts per million and gold at four parts per trillion.

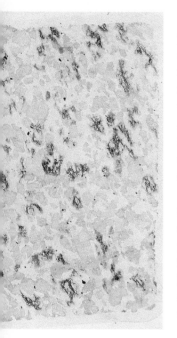

Thin section through gabbro. Most igneous rocks are complex mixtures of minerals which are too stable to be used as ores.

Three things are immediately apparent from this list. First, use of pure elements has little to do with their abundance – the oxygen in the air or the silicon used in chips are a minute fraction of the amounts which exist in chemical combination, while gold and uranium are eagerly sought after in spite of their rarity. Second, we unknowingly use most elements as chemical combinations – sand being the familiar form of silica (silicon oxide) and many rocks being complex 'aluminosilicates'. Third, even where elements are used in their pure form, the amounts used depend on how they are concentrated by natural processes and how easily they are purified chemically.

Most of the earth's crust is made up of igneous rocks (those which have solidified from a molten state), which all contain aluminosilicates of the abundant metals. Some of them, acid or granitic rocks, contain at least 50 per cent silica. These rocks are chemically rather stable, so even though they contain vast quantities of iron and aluminium they are not used as ores but only as rocks, for building or in crushed form for aggregate, road beds and so on. Workable ores result from natural concentrations of minerals which are more amenable to chemical purification.

Mineral distribution and trade

The three principal types of minerals in use, building materials, fossil fuels and metal ores, have very different patterns of distribution and trade. Building materials are used in huge quantities but most of them are of very low value and are only transported short distances. Fossil fuels and metal ores have more localised distributions, higher value and a more extensive pattern of international trade. Fossil fuels will be considered in the next chapter while this chapter concentrates on metals. As well over 95 per cent of world output of metals consists of iron, it is possible to describe mineral extraction and trade by concentrating on iron and then adding a few remarks about a small number of metals used in quite small quantities.

Iron is the fourth most abundant element in the crust and is concentrated in three ways. The highest grade ores, with more than 60 per cent iron, are 'magnetites', for example from Sweden, and 'haematites', such as those formerly mined in Cumbria. Though restricted in size, they are very pure and make up one third of world reserves. The most important sources of iron, half today's total, are the 'banded ironstones' from the oldest parts of the continents. The deposits are hundreds of metres thick and some extend hundreds of kilometres. They are much less pure and have to be milled, separated from the silica component and made into pellets for smelting; so they came into use later than other types of ore. The more recent sedimentary ores are low grade but were important in the early growth of industrialisation in Europe and North America. They are going

Figure 6.2 *Metals other than iron: production and reserve by country.*

	manganese	chromite[a]	nickel	cobalt	molybdenum[b]	tungsten	vanadium[c]	bauxite	magnesium	titanium	copper	tin	lead	zinc	gold	platinum[d]	silver	antimony[c]	mercury	cadmium[e]	uranium
Albania		▦																			
Algeria																			•		
Argentina																					
Australia	▦			•		•		R		R	•	•	R		•						R
Brazil		•				•				•				•	•						
Bolivia						•															
Canada			R	•	R					•			R		R	•	R		▦		R
Chile										R						•					
China	▦			•	•	R	▪	•	•	•	•	•		•	•	•		R	▦	•	
Cuba			•	•																	
Finland		•		•						•										•	
France						•		•	•											•	
Gabon	▦																				
Germany (FR)													•							•	
Greece			•					•													
Guinea																					
Hungary								•													
Indonesia			•									R									
Ireland													•								
Italy									•											•	
Jamaica								▨													
Korea (DR)					•								•	•							
Korea (Rep)					•															•	
Malaysia										•		▦									
Mexico	•				•						•		•	•			•	•	•		
Morocco													•								
Namibia																					▦
New Caledonia		▦																			
Niger																					•
Norway								▦													
Papua											•				•						
Peru			•	•						R		•						•		•	
Poland											•			•		•				•	
Philippines			•	•							•		•		•						
South Africa	R	R	•			R				•	•	•		•	•	▨	R	•			▦
Spain											•		•					R			
Sweden											•		•								
Thailand											R							•			
Yugoslavia							•				•		R	•							
USA					R	•	•	▤			▪		•	•			R				
USSR	▤	▦									▦				R	▤	R		R		
Zaïre				▤																	
Zambia																					

Percentage of total production

• 2–6	▪ 12–21	▨ 32–41
▦ 7–11	▨ 22–31	▤ 42–55

R Major source of reserves

a Chromite is always found with other metals (usually iron) as an oxide.
b Molybdenum is sometimes produced as a by-product of copper.
c Vanadium and antimony are produced only as by-products of other metals.
d Only South Africa and the USSR mine platinum in its own right.
e Cadmium is found with lead-zinc ores.

out of use now that bulk carriers can move higher grade ores half way across the world. Blast furnaces and steelworks can be run at any port site where efficient production and local demand make it profitable to do so. It also means that pollution from smelters is more likely to be found in industrial areas than at the source of the ore.

The major sources of metals other than iron are shown in Figure 6.2. It is apparent that about half of these metals have over one-third of world production coming from a single country. What is not apparent from this figure is the domination of production and trade by transnational companies. Just as the oil industry is dominated by seven corporations, so six dominate aluminium trade, two dominate nickel and three uranium. Past attempts by governments of less developed countries such as Zaire, Zambia and Peru to expropriate or tax mining operations run by transnationals have led to a concentration of exploration into politically 'safe' countries. In fact 80 per cent of 'free world' exploration effort is expended in the USA, Canada, Australia and South Africa and very little now occurs in less developed countries.

Finally, it should be noted that some of these metals, notably aluminium, manganese, magnesium, chrome and titanium, are geologically abundant so, in spite of substantial and growing production, there are few problems of supply. The other metals are scarcer, which leads at best to the use of lean ores – down to half per cent for copper ores – and at worst to actual and potential shortages, as with silver, tungsten and tin. The results for the environment are damaging – large voids and spoil heaps, use of large amounts of energy in extraction and pressure to exploit existing deposits to the maximum.

▷ **Bauxite mining in the Amazon. Many tropical areas have deep laterite soils produced by breakdown of bedrock by percolating water. Some are rich in alumina and are mined, adding another pressure on tropical forests.**

Environmental impacts of mineral exploitation

The impacts of mineral exploitation are varied and complex. As shown in Figure 6.3, they occur at every stage of the mineral cycle, from extraction, through processing and use to disposal as waste. They differ between substances used as construction materials, chemicals, metals and fuels. A crucial point at which to start is that while the obvious impacts are physical (for example, noise and dust) most of the really damaging impacts are chemical, because the processing of naturally occurring minerals involves and produces many elements and compounds, some of which are toxic. These substances are entering air, land and water and affecting the health of plants, animals and people.

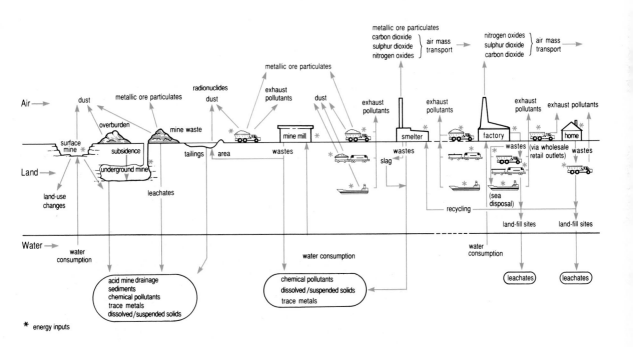

Figure 6.3 *Impacts of mineral extraction and use.*

Extraction

The impacts of mineral extraction are mostly physical, but with one crucial exception: acid drainage. The most apparent impact is made by extraction of large volumes of minerals, especially when it occurs close to settled areas.

In the UK, more complaints about environmental disruption concern sand and gravel pits than anything else. This is because such pits are very extensive in relation to amounts of materials and have to be close to their markets, which are often in urban areas. Noise, dust and increased traffic are the principal problems. Although the number of active sites has decreased, the volumes produced continue to increase and thousands of hectares are designated for future use. Regulation has concentrated on after care to restore the landscape and/or use it for water based recreation.

Demand for coarse aggregate for road and building construction has put increased pressure on quarries where harder rocks are extracted. Use of building stone and slate has declined, but limestone continues to be used in large volumes for agricultural lime, cement manufacture and by the chemical industry. Recently, limestone quarries in the Mendips, Charnwood Forest and the Pennines have begun to supply crushed stone for construction in the south east of England. The result is increased pressure on areas heavily used for recreation.

Open-cast coal mining, Ruhr, Germany. Use of massive machinery allows stripping of overburden and economic mining of underlying seams. In the foreground overburden is being spread prior to reclamation.

Coal mining is another activity which involves very large volumes of waste, especially because mechanised production in underground mines produces double the spoil of manual production and open-cast production is even more disruptive. At present it is estimated that every 70 million tonnes of coal will require an additional 200 hectares for spoil dumping. Around 10,000 hectares of Britain have already been used for open-cast coal extraction, though such areas are soon rehabilitated. In the Ruhr, open-cast mines have temporarily displaced 25,000 people and transformed 19,000 hectares. World-wide, about half of the output of coal (currently 3,500 million tonnes) is obtained from open-cast workings.

In one respect, underground mining of coal can have more serious impacts than surface mining: subsidence can damage buildings, transport routes and drainage networks. The USA is one of the few countries where overall estimates are available, revealing that 32,000 square kilometres have already been affected, with another 10,000 square kilometres expected by the end of the century. The incidence of subsidence can be reduced, but this means leaving substantial quantities of coal *in situ*. In the UK, salt extraction has caused subsidence of up to half a metre over hundreds of hectares. Early methods used boreholes to pump in water and extract brine with no regard for subsidence. More recent use of controlled pumping can reduce the problem. World-wide, oil extraction has caused significant problems of subsidence, the effects of which are worst in low lying coastal locations like Long Beach, California. So serious is the damage there that over $100 million has been spent constructing dykes and attempting to repressurise the oil bearing strata with water.

One of the most widespread effects of mineral extraction is a chemical change: the creation of acid drainage waters. The fragmentation of rocks has two main effects. First, it increases the penetration of air and water. Second, it increases the total surface area of the rock – the finer the particles, the greater the surface area. When sulphides are present, they react with the oxygen in air and with water to produce the equivalent of dilute sulphuric acid. This more acid drainage water passing over the large surface area of the particles dissolves metals including toxic ones like cadmium and lead. Because many of the large-scale mines which produce acid drainage are in remote areas, like the interior of Canada, their effects are not researched as intensively as the effects of acid rain, but it is clear that a shift in water acidity will have damaging effects on ecosystems even without a lacing of toxic heavy metals.

Chemical processing

Many minerals, from limestone to most metal ores and petroleum, are chemically processed to produce a desirable product, whether a pure metal

The Hope Valley cement works can be seen from many of the upland areas of the Peak District National Park.

or a compound, or mixture of compounds like fertilisers. This chemical processing has a variety of impacts from cosmetic to lethal.

In Britain, much controversy has been generated by the Hope cement works in the heart of the Peak National Park. This uses 1.75 million tonnes of limestone a year, together with local shale and gypsum, is fuelled by coal from outside the park and produces about one-tenth of Britain's cement. Some 80 million tonnes of limestone have consent for quarrying, implying that the plant will continue to operate for several decades. In this case, the impact is from dust, smoke and damage to amenity land.

In other cases, processing may use a variety of chemicals. Among metals, aluminium is a particularly problematic case. Pure alumina is extracted from bauxite with caustic soda, leaving a residue of fine red mud contaminated with caustic soda and fluorides – about 40 million tonnes a year in the 1980s. Emissions to the air include sulphur dioxide and hydrogen fluoride as well as greenhouse gases like carbon dioxide and ozone depleting carbon tetrafluoride. So, even though the final purification of aluminium metal is by electrolysis, and limited in its impacts, purification of the ore is environmentally damaging.

Smelting of most metals involves furnaces which remove oxygen from oxides by reduction with coke, a process which also produces carbon dioxide, heat and dust. We have already seen that the prior roasting of sulphide ores to produce oxides adds emissions of metal particles and sulphur dioxide and results in acid rain. A particularly carefully researched problem is poisoning by eating foodstuffs produced near cadmium smelters. Research in Japan showed that *itai itai* disease resulted from ingestion of cadmium, which was present at 18 parts per million in plants near one smelter. As a result, the use of cadmium was banned in Japan. However, it continues in England, the USA, Australia and Canada. In a rare case of marine pollution, several dozen people were killed by eating fish caught in Japan's Minamata Bay in the early 1970s. Mercury discharged from a factory had been taken up by plants, concentrated in the food chain and made fish highly toxic.

Just as much to blame as the chemical processing of metal ores has been the chemical industry itself. From its earliest stages (for example in Cheshire in the 1830s and 1840s) when gaseous hydrogen chloride was released into the air, killing vegetation for miles around, to its vast and sophisticated extent today (when the Federal Government of the USA records some 12,000 different chemical wastes of which about one-sixth are carcinogenic) the chemical industry has been both a boon to society and a threat to the environment. Indeed, it caused the world's worst industrial accident when, on the night of 3 December 1984, a release of methyl isocyanate gas killed several thousand people and crippled tens of thousands of others at Bhopal, India. The chemical industry is too complex a topic for a book like this, but it is clear that accidents and careless disposal of toxic wastes have already had incalculable impacts on people and the environment. Nowhere is the double edged nature of modern technology more apparent, for this is also an industry which makes possible a host of industrial processes and which produces the massive amounts of fertiliser which have expanded agricultural output. Indeed, the Union Carbide plant at Bhopal was producing fertiliser.

The modern chemical industry is increasingly using petroleum as a starting point, but the vast majority of petroleum is still used to produce fuels, from heavy oils to aviation spirit. The negative outcomes of the whole process of mineral use make it essential to look at safe disposal of waste products and at reducing impacts right through the cycle.

Impacts from wastes

For thousand of years human society has used the environment as a sink for its wastes as well as a source of raw materials. When the wastes were limited in quantity and organic in origin, few serious problems resulted. Now that so much waste is of mineral origin, and often in unstable and even toxic forms, the problems are much more serious. They affect air, land and water.

A variety of forms of air pollution have already been mentioned, ranging from dust, metal particles and smoke to gases like sulphur dioxide and nitrogen oxides. The latter will be discussed in more detail in later chapters. A particular air pollutant which is relevant here is lead from vehicle exhausts. This has been known for many years to cause brain damage and behavioural disorders in children living near major roads. However, little was done in the UK because it was argued that the public would not accept the banning of lead additives which improve the performance of cars. It was only when fears of acid rain posed a more general challenge to vehicle use that the UK government moved to encourage use of lead free fuel through differential taxation, with the medium-term aim of allowing use of catalytic convertors.

The massive cost of rehabilitating the derelict site of the Shelton Bar steelworks in Stoke could only be met by making this one of a series of garden festivals.

Pollution of land is evident in old industrial districts and in dumps. There are thousands of hectares of derelict land in Britain, as there are in other areas with long industrial histories. Decades of building and rebuilding, leaks and dumping of process materials and wastes have rendered these areas difficult and expensive to re-use. The huge investment required to prepare the Garden Festival sites at Stoke, Liverpool, Glasgow and Gateshead is an indication of the problem. Equally damaging has been the

practice in the past of allowing industrial waste to be dumped on household waste sites without recording what went where. Even well run and well documented toxic waste dumps, ideally on impermeable sites, such as clay, are a permanent problem. Still worse are the inadequate dumps in less developed countries which accepted other countries' waste for fees which, while far below the costs of controlled disposal in Europe, represented a massive increase to the GNP. Indeed, Guinea Bissau was offered $120 million to accept 15 million tonnes of waste – an amount equal to its total GNP. The Italian waste, temporarily 'stored' at Koko Beach in Nigeria and then brought to Britain in the Karin B, made the public aware of the growing trade in hazardous waste, but did little to solve the problem. While such waste continues to be produced, the issue will remain as to whether it should be permanently dumped in landfill sites or whether it can be destroyed by high temperature incineration. At present, public concern over possible contamination from incinerators, whether on land or in the North Sea, seems to outweigh concerns over the permanent storage of 'cocktails' of chemicals which may eventually leak into water systems.

Water pollution from mines, spoil heaps and acid rain has already been discussed. In the UK these sources are less important than two and possibly three others. The doubtful one is leachates from dumps: if rain is allowed to soak into dumps containing toxic materials, it can dissolve them and carry them into streams. Current dumps are managed to prevent this, but many hundreds of former dumps exist where this problem could arise. Much better known are the releases from industrial premises. Fortunately, the UK has not suffered any incidents like the one at the Sandoz plant in Basle in 1986, where a release of pesticides and insecticides killed 500,000 fish as it travelled down the Rhine. However, there are still hundreds of incidents a year where permitted levels of discharge are exceeded and those levels already mean that some rivers are almost devoid of life. In the last decade a new source of water pollution has begun to rival industry. Agriculture now uses large quantities of minerals, some of which – weedkillers and pesticides – are intentionally toxic to plants and insects. Early products, as revealed by Rachel Carson's classic book *Silent Spring*, were often persistent and could be concentrated in the food chain to levels fatal for many predatory birds. More selective and less persistent chemicals are used today in more developed countries, but some dangerous products are still in use in less developed countries. So ubiquitous have some chemicals become that even Antarctic penguins have been found to have DDT in their bodies. Indeed, it has been estimated that we each eat about 5 kg of chemical residues and food additives a year. Added to this are mounting levels of nitrate residues in water, with some areas of the UK exceeding EC recommended levels.

Except in extreme cases, it is unclear what this increasing exposure to low levels of contamination is doing to human populations or the environment. This is a debate which could become as contentious as the debate on air and water pollution from the nuclear reprocessing plant at Sellafield. Since the plant was set up in 1948 to produce plutonium for nuclear bombs, there have been substantial releases of a variety of radioactive materials, both accidental (notably in the reactor fire of 1957) and deliberate (especially via the pipeline to the Irish Sea). Discharges in the 1960s and 1970s were high enough to bring local shellfish eaters and houseboat residents very near the then permitted doses, which have subsequently been reduced. The discovery in the 1980s of clusters of leukaemia cases near Sellafield and other nuclear facilities at Burghfield and Dounreay triggered a debate which is still not completely resolved, although it currently looks as if the cause may be exposure of workers in the plants rather than of people in the surrounding area. Routine discharges are now at a very low level but the accumulation of radioactive waste is an increasing problem to which no long-term solution has been found. The most likely treatment of intermediate level waste is an underground repository below Sellafield – a solution dictated by the political opposition to other proposed sites for nuclear waste.

Reducing the impacts of mineral processing

The UK, as the first industrialised nation, has a long history of attempts to reduce industrial pollution, stimulated partly by increasing smoke emissions and partly by chemical releases. The result has been a complex system, with a mass of legislation and several regulatory agencies. Regulation has often been tentative because of lack of appropriate technology and financial concerns. More recently, membership of the EC has brought a new approach to regulation, but there remains a problem of adopting the policies of prevention, recycling and substitution because the cost implications may damage firms' competitive ability.

Growing industrial pollution in the nineteenth century brought a double response. The Smoke Control Acts were developed for control of local nuisances and administered by local government. Two Alkali Acts, regulating chemical discharges, were administered by the Alkali Inspectorate. This was a centrally financed body, staffed by technically competent people who would visit chemical firms and negotiate pollution reductions in the light of what was technically and financially possible. The dominant philosophy has come to be called 'best practical means' (BPM) because it rejected imposing arbitrary standards. However, critics have argued that the close identification of inspectors with industry had the effect of softening the regulations.

Since 1945 there has been a further expansion of legislation dealing with pollution, but the double, central/local system has been maintained. The planning system set up in 1947 gave local authorities powers to approve or disapprove proposals for industrial development. The position of the Alkali Inspectorate was maintained, but supplemented by a range of controls brought together in the Health and Safety at Work Act and administered by the Health and Safety Executive (HSE). Subsequently the Notification of Installations Handling Hazardous Substances (NIHHS) Regulations 1982 and the Control of Industrial Major Accident Hazards (CIMAH) Regulations 1984 were added to the HSE's brief. So complex had the system of regulation become, it was no surprise that in 1987 the Government decided to bring together the Alkali, Hazardous Wastes, Radiochemical and Water Inspectorates as Her Majesty's Inspectorate of Pollution – a unified central body for pollution control. Unfortunately the unity was soon lost as proposals for privatising the water industry produced a separate National Rivers Authority (NRA) to regulate water pollution. The early indications are that the NRA has been restricted in its ability to make the water companies comply with water quality standards.

The principles underlying EC rules are quite different from Britain's BPM principle. The EC aims to set Environmental Quality Standards in the light of evidence, for example from the World Health Organisation, on health hazards. It then imposes Emission Limits designed to achieve the standards. The aim is to create a 'level playing field' for competition by imposing the same standards on all firms. The so-called Green Bill of 1990 seems to be a truly British compromise, defining a new principle – Best Practicable Environmental Option (BPEO) – which seems to continue the spirit of BPM, while making it possible for the minister to impose Emission Limits set by the EC – standards which are expected to tighten progressively in the future. The Bill also recognises a principle which originated in Germany and which could have radical implications. The 'prevention principle' recognises that rather than limit pollution and clean up retrospectively, it will often be much more effective to prevent the pollution from occurring in the first place. But how could this be done?

Recycling and substitution

Earlier sections of this chapter identified a range of worsening problems arising from mineral extraction and use. In some cases the impacts increase even faster because shortages of the purest ores require use of leaner ores, with higher energy requirements, bigger voids and larger amounts of waste. Such problems, which arise most obviously in the case of metals, can be reduced by substitution and/or recycling.

A classic case of substitution is in electrical uses of copper. Early this century copper was used for all electrical wiring including transatlantic cables. Since then the relative scarcity and consequent high price of copper have led to substitution. Aluminium was a suitable substitute in cables, but the demand for metal cables has been reduced by the use of optical-fibre cables over short distances, microwave transmitters at medium scale and satellites over the longer distances. These substitutes use fewer, cheaper or more abundant minerals but have one major problem. Although more efficient in use of materials, they are more energy intensive and hence put pressure on two of the minerals in finite supply: coal and petroleum. Similar problems arise from the substitution of plastics (which are mostly made from oil) for metal. A more promising strategy for the future is to use more ceramics, since clay is abundantly available.

Recycling looks an even more promising strategy since re-use of materials can simultaneously solve problems of mining, refining and disposal. At best, for example in the case of the re-use of aluminium or glass, it is also much less energy intensive. Indeed, recycling is so obviously advantageous that it is surprising that only between one-quarter and one-third of metals output uses recycled materials. At present, the problem lies in the great complexity of products like cars. Not only do they involve metals other than steel, but they include many different kinds of steel. A recycled batch of steel may contain appreciable quantities of chromium, cobalt, manganese, nickel, tungsten and/or vanadium. These become impurities which make its behaviour unpredictable and at present no practical technology exists to remove them. As a result, scrap has to be combined with new steel and confined to low grade uses. Similar problems arise with aluminium: recycled aluminium is insufficiently pure to use for wire or sheet. Unfortunately, demand for cast aluminium is not high at present. No doubt these kinds of problems could be resolved but at present the financial incentives are not strong enough to persuade industry to make the necessary commitments to new technology and more expensive processes.

Taxation

Since the rapid increase of impacts on the environment results from the pursuit of economic goals, it is being increasingly argued that, rather than exhort industrialists or fine them for breaches of environmental regulations, governments should develop taxation structures which penalise environmentally damaging activities and reward desirable ones. In the UK the leading exponent of this view has been Professor David Pearce in his

Blueprint for a Green Economy. However, though the 'polluter pays' principle is now widely quoted, the differential tax on leaded and unleaded petrol appears to be the only explicit use of taxation to promote good practice. Other countries in Europe and Scandinavia have been a little more ambitious, especially in trying to establish 'carbon taxes' to reduce consumption of fossil fuels, but even there progress is slow.

If the problem is difficult in a single country, it is even more difficult on a world-wide basis, which is where it ultimately needs to be tackled. Developed countries tend to have more stringent regulation and much higher levels of consumption. Less developed countries have avoided strong controls partly to avoid offending transnational corporations and partly because they aspire to higher consumption of material goods. But if poor countries (currently consuming between 10 and 50 kg of steel per head per year) were to raise their consumption to that of the OECD average (currently over 400 kg per head) steel output would have to quadruple. Even if this were technically possible, it would be environmentally damaging.

A final complication is that the principle of stewardship requires us to avoid actions which will penalise future generations. It is clear that the dissipation of scarce resources and the storage of toxic and radioactive wastes both contravene this principle. But how should they be costed and how could taxation and international agreements act on behalf of future generations? This is a problem which relates to the whole environment rather than just mineral exploitation. It is the main focus of Chapter 9.

CHAPTER 7

Energy: a renewable future?

'Energy efficiency can only buy time for the world to develop "low
energy paths" based on renewable sources, which should form the
foundation of the global energy structure during the twenty-first
century ... It is clear that a low energy path is the best way towards
a sustainable future.'

Our Common Future, 1987.

Energy, like minerals, is talked of in terms of being a 'primary resource' but it is altogether distinctive, although both are clearly related. Some important energy resources, such as coal, oil and uranium, are themselves minerals; and the extraction and processing of minerals requires energy, in a suitable form, to drive digging and crushing machinery and to modify chemical structure, as in the process of smelting ores to produce useful metals.

In the previous chapter we were concerned with the environmental effects of mining and the processing of minerals, and with policies for the rehabilitation of damaged landscapes and the control of associated pollution. Here we are tackling what for many environmentalists is one of the most critical global issues of all, the production and consumption of energy and the associated undesirable environmental effects, from smog, acid rain and oil spills to Chernobyl and global warming. The international debate on global warming and the need to limit the emission of harmful 'greenhouse gases', notably carbon dioxide (CO_2), particularly from the burning of fossil fuels like coal and oil, is the focus for discussion in the next chapter.

▲ **Constructing the Sarcophagus at Chernobyl following the explosion in April 1986.**

The idea of energy options for the future is central to our discussion in this chapter. But to arrive at any meaningful assessment of 'choice' or 'practicable policy alternatives' requires consideration of a number of interrelated issues: the relationship between supply and demand – the production of power from a variety of energy sources and global patterns of consumption; the balance between renewable and non-renewable energy resources; changing patterns of use in the more developed world and increasing energy requirements in the less developed world; energy efficiency, resource conservation and the exploration of new energy paths for the world to follow. To help us along the way we shall be looking at energy policies in Denmark, a country that has adopted a progressive approach in catering for its energy needs. However, first we should take a broad view of the global energy picture.

Global energy resources and use

One of the most crucial areas of concern for environmentalists is the extent to which all nations are prepared, or able, to move from relying predominantly on non-renewable energy resources – fossil fuels and nuclear fuels – to an increasing use of 'renewable' resources – solar, wind, tidal power. The conventional starting point for looking at energy resources globally is to examine the way in which the proved reserves of fossil fuels are distributed around the world, for at the start of the 1990s global energy needs continued to be dominated by coal, oil and natural gas.

◀ **Previous page**
Fiddlers Ferry coal fired power station near Widnes, Cheshire. This is one of several power stations to be fitted with desulphurisation equipment to reduce pollution.

Britain's industrial revolution was based upon ready access to coal, which soon became equally important world-wide, as it still is. In the USA at the end of the nineteenth century, oil also became vital, supporting the development of the automobile, soon to become a world issue in its own right. In the mid-twentieth century the use of natural gas as a cleaner domestic and industrial fuel increased throughout the developed world. Figures 7.1, 7.2 and 7.3 provide an indication of the proved reserves of these three primary resources in 1989. As Reddish (1991) comments, 'current perceptions of the amounts of these fuels now available give an instant image of powerful economic and political influences at work at the end of the twentieth century'.

Figures 7.1–7.3 were produced by the oil industry. They show the map of the world redrawn with the different regions scaled in proportion to their proved reserves of oil, gas and coal. The amounts indicated need to be treated with caution. 'Proved reserves' refers only to those resources judged to be extractable 'under existing economic and operating conditions' and not to the amounts that might be ultimately available. So the concept of reserves depends on the state of exploration and extraction technology, and on world prices, which in turn depend on the main operators in the energy industries.

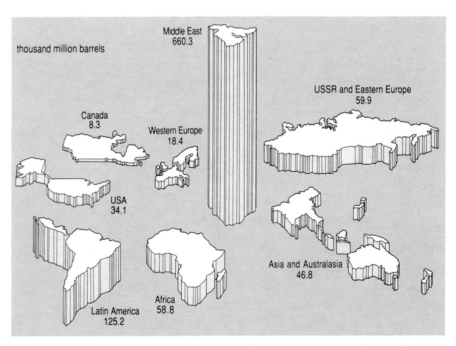

Figure 7.1 *Global proved reserves of oil, 1989. The conventional map has been redrawn in three-dimensional form to highlight the dominant position of the Middle East.*
Redrawn from BP Statistical Review of World Energy, British Petroleum Company, 1990.

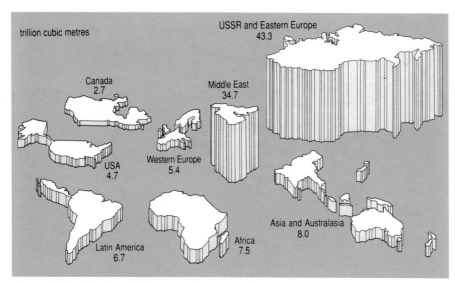

Figure 7.2 *Global proved reserves of natural gas, 1989. Here the USSR and the Middle East dominate the world map.*
Redrawn from BP Statistical Review of World Energy, British Petroleum Company, 1990.

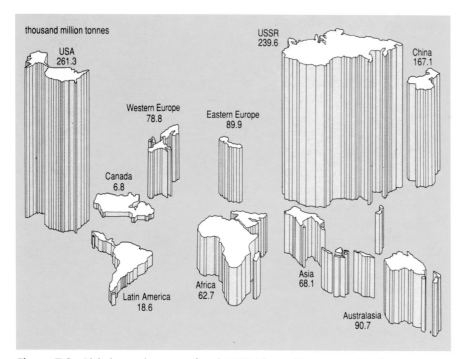

Figure 7.3 *Global proved reserves of coal, 1989. The world's reserves of coal are more evenly distributed than either oil or natural gas. However, the USA, the USSR and China have far larger reserves than any other area.*
Redrawn from BP Statistical Review of World Energy, British Petroleum Company, 1990.

The oil slick in the Persian Gulf, as seen by the US Landsat remote sensing satellite on 16 February 1991. The slick, highlighted in red for easy viewing, extends approximately 64 km into the southern extent of the bay near the Saudi island of Abu Ali.

Their influence was no better demonstrated than in the oil crisis of 1973, when the Middle East-dominated cartel OPEC (Organisation of Petroleum Exporting Countries) ensured that restricting supplies became a highly profitable venture. Indeed, Figure 7.1 graphically displays the continuing overwhelming dominance of that region in terms of supplies of oil, which is a major factor of political instability. Iraq's invasion of Kuwait in 1990 and the subsequent Gulf War in 1991 were potent and horrifying reminders of the measures that some nations, for differing reasons, are prepared to take to 'safeguard' essential supplies of a basic resource. In the event, estimates of proven reserves will have to be revised following the fires that burned out of control throughout Kuwait. The environmental costs of that episode have been truly enormous.

Of course, what Figures 7.1–7.3 do not show is the relation of these reserves to world demand. In 1988 it was estimated that at current extraction rates oil supplies would last for 42 years, if averaged over the whole world, ranging from five years for the United Kingdom and 10 for North America to over 100 years for several Middle Eastern states. For natural gas the estimates were scarcely more encouraging, with an average world 'life expectancy' of 55 years, ranging from over 100 years for the Middle East to only 13 years for the UK and North America. The fossil fuel with the longest life span is coal, the original industrial fuel. Its world-wide distribution is more even than either oil or natural gas and at current consumption rates it could be at least the twenty-third century, and probably beyond, before known supplies are used up.

Allowing for the fact that all such projections should be viewed circumspectly, these figures nevertheless highlight one very significant part of the energy problem, the continuing dependence on fossil fuels by the majority of countries, whether less or more developed, and the reluctance of coal-rich countries to see any constraints placed upon the burning of coal, one of the principal contributors to the greenhouse effect. As Figure 7.3 shows, North America, the USSR and China are all richly endowed with coal reserves.

Global patterns of consumption are just as significant. Figure 7.4 shows the total consumption of primary energy for the non-communist world 1970–1989. Excluded from these data are biomass fuels – wood, animal wastes – essential to the fuel requirements of many less developed nations (they are not traded and therefore do not appear in commercial statistics) and other forms of renewable energy too small to register on this diagram. Biomass fuels are believed to provide 10–15 per cent of the world's primary energy needs, which gives some indication of the pressure on forest resources of indigenous peoples, an issue referred to in Chapter 3.

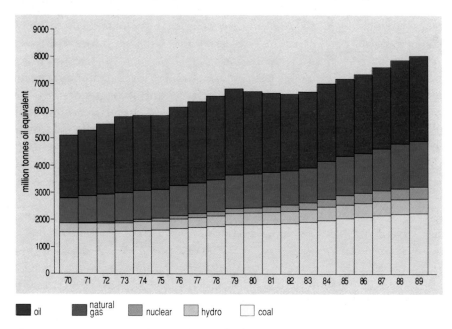

Figure 7.4 Consumption of primary energy for the non-communist world, 1970–1989. Redrawn from BP Statistical Review of World Energy, British Petroleum Company, 1990.

The key point is that energy has been used and continues to be used in most parts of the world in an unsustainable manner, with demand being distributed quite unequally. About 25 per cent of the world's people consume over 75 per cent of the world's primary energy. Yet, even within the more developed world, energy is being consumed at variable rates, from about 4–5 kilowatts per capita in Europe and Japan through to about 10 kW per capita in the United States. Consumption is less than 1 kW per head in many less developed countries, but from the developing world demand is increasing all the time, partly as a factor of population growth, but more specifically related to an urgent desire to industrialise. If the growing world population follows the development path of industrialised countries, the pressure on existing energy resources will be overwhelming.

The unequal energy habits of different nations are highlighted by the dominance of the United States in the use of oil, gas and coal. In 1988 oil accounted for some 38 per cent of US commercial energy consumption, with oil imports amounting to over 40 million dollars' worth, approximately equivalent to one-third of the nation's trade deficit. The US transportation system alone consumes enough oil to provide for all Japan's energy needs. The sheer scale of energy consumption in the United States indicates that the US could have a major impact on global carbon emissions by developing more efficient cost-effective technologies. But is this likely to happen and if so, when?

The international community faces a daunting challenge in attempting to set targets for the reduction of global emissions from the continuing use of fossil fuels, let alone enforcing them. But where should the principal responsibilities rest for tackling the major problems? Is it feasible to shift dependence from non-renewable to renewable sources, and whilst this is being achieved to stretch existing energy supplies through energy efficient technologies, without exhausting those supplies and without having further recourse to the controversial and potentially hazardous generation of nuclear power? That is a tall order indeed, more especially for less developed countries that are heavily dependent upon 'dirty' and inefficient technology. However, one nation in Northern Europe is hoping to set an example that others can follow – Denmark.

Danish energy – a sustainable approach?

Denmark is too small a country, with a population in the region of five million, to have much direct impact on the global nature of the energy problem, but it may be able to demonstrate sustainable ways of meeting industrial and domestic demands for energy that will be helpful to the more developed and less developed world alike. Danish energy policy sets out to satisfy industrial and social needs whilst remaining aware of the environmental problems that the demand for energy can create. It is based upon two precepts: the more efficient use of existing sources of energy and a gradual shift to renewable sources.

Traditionally, Denmark has had to import virtually all its energy requirements, having no indigenous fossil fuel reserves. In 1990, 95 per cent of electricity was generated from coal, a large proportion of which came from Colombia in Latin America. The current dependence on coal stems from the 1973 oil crisis, when oil prices quadrupled and put a serious drain on Denmark's foreign exchange because of the country's overwhelming reliance on oil. Coal is still the cheapest fuel available and the Danish utility companies have been able to negotiate favourable contracts with developing countries. It is also cheap, explains Professor Neils Meyer of the National Technical University, because '[The companies] don't pay the costs (the environmental costs) inflicted on society'.

This is a recognition of the damaging effects of continuing to use a conventional energy source and of the need for some realistic accounting of the environmental costs, but at least the fuel is used efficiently. At Odense, Denmark's second city, a modern coal-fired power station is typical, differing from nearly all UK power stations in the fully established use of 'combined heat and power generation' (CHP). Hot water is pumped to almost every building in the city, commercial and residential, in a centralised district heating system. The heat is taken out in the individual buildings by means of heat exchangers and the cooled water is returned to the power station for reheating, thus dispensing with the need for cooling towers. In terms of efficiency, the energy saved in this operation is equivalent to the capacity of another power station.

▲ *A modern coal powered electricity generating station in Denmark. (The absence of smoke does not mean the absence of harmful gases that continue to be emitted into the atmosphere.)*

However, coal burning produces pollution, both in the traditional sense of smoke and dust and also in the sulphur dioxide and nitrogen oxides associated with acid rain production. There are solutions in the form of good combustion engineering, but at a price. In addition, the carbon dioxide necessarily produced in fossil fuel combustion is of increasing concern for its contribution to global warming, an issue taken up in the next chapter.

Consequently, the Danes are progressively reducing their reliance on any single energy source and are gradually replacing coal at Odense with natural gas from the North Sea. Gas is intrinsically cleaner than coal and also produces less carbon dioxide for a given amount of energy. So current power station policy involves a considerable changeover to gas in CHP plants and a move towards smaller, decentralised stations. Figure 7.5 overleaf shows the changing pattern of energy use from 1973–1990.

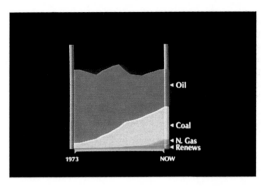

Figure 7.5 *Changing patterns of energy use in Denmark, 1973–1990.*
BBC/OU Productions, U206 Environment, *graphics from TV6 'Danish Energy', 1991.*

There is no policy to use nuclear power, although it was an obvious option here given the lack of fossil fuels. It was certainly feasible during the 1960s, but a plentiful supply of cheap oil meant that the nuclear option was shelved. During the 1970s public awareness grew and heated debate and well organised public protest finally led to a government decision in 1984 to reject it formally. This was based on two key factors: the safety argument and detailed proposals from the Organisation Opposing Atomic power (OOA) for an alternative energy strategy.

Energy alternatives

The OOA proposals were based upon an integrated energy and environment analysis, the objective of which was to increase the potential choices available in providing reliable and continuing sources of energy on a sustainable basis. The Alternative Energy Plan emphasises two basic principles:

1   Energy conservation to reduce total energy demand.

2   Renewable sources of energy increasingly to replace the conventional sources, but only in tandem with policies for conservation.

Although Danish national policy already goes further in these directions than most other countries do, there is still a divergence between what the Government sees as realistic and the 'alternative' projections. This is shown in Figure 7.6. While the Government expects total energy use to increase by 2000, with a growing use of gas and a modest increase in renewables, the alternative plan argues for a halving of total use by 2000 and reduction to

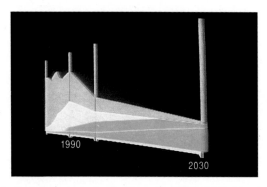

Figure 7.6 *Projected energy use in Denmark, 1990–2030, based on OOA alternative proposals.*
BBC/OU Productions, U206 Environment, graphics from TV6 'Danish Energy', 1991.

one-quarter by 2030, with a growing dominance of renewables and coal being phased out altogether. This is clearly an ambitious approach, but is it attainable?

Supporters of the Alternative Energy Plan are convinced that it is and point to a series of technological developments and current projects that underline both the efficiency and conservation arguments and the requirements to shift progressively to the use of renewables. In terms of new technology, it is being widely demonstrated that significant energy savings can be made by investing in low energy domestic appliances, like refrigerators which use one-quarter of the electricity of conventional models and fluorescent lighting. Although the initial cost is higher, they are still cost effective because of the huge potential for energy conservation. Also, existing house insulation standards are considerably higher than they are in the UK and even further improvements are being sought.

All of this requires a long-term commitment on the part of government and industry, but nevertheless these are the kinds of technical change that, followed through in detail, could lead to the projected reductions in total energy demand contained in the alternative plan. Relying on technological innovation is only part of the equation, however. Denmark is already active in promoting ways of meeting demand from renewable sources. Two in particular are worthy of note. Both are based upon traditional ideas, but make use of the latest technology: the production of methane gas and wind power.

Experimental projects are already well in hand to produce methane from pig slurry, using an 'anaerobic digester'. The methane is then used as a fuel for a local power and heating system. This type of solution is well suited to local, decentralised systems of power generation and is a good example of using biomass as an energy source, applicable equally to wood

▷ **A wind farm in Denmark.**

and straw burning or the use of the energy remaining in domestic refuse. Pig meat is Denmark's largest single export so there is a correspondingly high density of animal waste available.

Denmark has long pioneered the development of wind turbines and their mass production is now a competitive proposition, based upon a robust technology. The latest designs are capable of generating 400–500 kilowatts of electricity. In 1990 there were around 2,000 mills in Denmark, contributing a little over one per cent of the total electricity supply, but such is the scale of development that experts are confidently predicting a tenfold increase in output by the year 2000. Resistance to change has come from the utility companies, but there is continuing pressure from the Government to see wind power as an increasingly significant and viable alternative. Ultimately, development may be limited by the variability of the resource (the wind) itself to meeting some 20 per cent of national demand.

It is quite apparent that wind power is no longer a speculative option in Denmark. However, there will be a need for other techniques to become as practical and economic as the wind turbine – for example, the direct use

◁ **The largest solar powered water heating system in the world, in Sweden.**

of solar energy for heat and electricity production, wave and tidal power –
if the objective of near total reliance on renewable sources is to be realised.
Denmark is keenly alert to these possibilities; but in global terms how
significant are this small country's efforts (with just 0.1 per cent of the world
population) to promote energy efficiency and the use of alternative, renewable
sources?

The scope for global solutions

For all its efforts Denmark still relies predominantly on energy habits that
are globally damaging. Dependency on coal brought in from developing
countries is not good for improving the global environment. The
encouragement resides less in what has been achieved than in the potential
for what could be achieved by 2000 and beyond. The increasing preparedness
of industrialised countries to switch progressively to energy technologies
that are environmentally benign signals a certain level of commitment to
the less developed world. For even dramatic improvements in energy
efficiency and shifts to renewable sources will not be sufficient to protect the
environment if they are confined to the industrialised world alone.

Yet herein lies the real crux of the debate about global energy demands
and use and the impact on the environment. Whose problems are they? As
we have noted already, the industrialised world consumes the lion's share
of energy resources. A particularly quotable quote is that 'the United States
has consumed more fossil fuels and minerals in the past 50 years than the
rest of humanity in the whole of recorded history' (Sandy Irvine 'No growth
in a finite world', *New Statesman*, 23 November 1990). The industrialised
world has the tools at hand, as the case study of Denmark has demonstrated,
to increase efficiency and decrease the use of fossil fuels; but has it the
political will or the capacity for enlightened economic thinking to do so
where it really counts?

The less developed world's energy consumption is small; but it is
inefficient and demand is growing rapidly. Developing countries clearly
face some hard choices but should the richer nations that have already
reaped the benefits of many decades of economic development be telling the
poorer nations how they can or cannot develop? If we take the cases of India
and China, together they account for two-fifths of the world's population
and both are following paths towards industrialisation, if in somewhat
different political economic circumstances. Nevertheless, both nations are
seeking the sort of material benefits that are associated with economic
growth and development. It is the expressed aim of the Chinese authorities
to have a refrigerator in every home by 2000.

It has been calculated that the path to industrial development in China alone could have a greater effect on the atmospheric accumulation of carbon dioxide than that of any other nation. Industrial processes have a tendency towards being energy intensive and inefficient and there is a huge reliance on coal, of which China is the world's largest producer, as shown in Figure 7.3. China's manufacturing sector grew by an average of 12 per cent per annum during the 1980s, the fastest growth in any large country in the world, and the energy intensity of that sector remains higher than the intensity of any other developing nation. This has led some leading analysts in the West to conclude that the great potential for improved efficiency is China's principal future energy resource.

That is all well and good but what grounds are there for arguing that China is likely to take the 'energy efficient path', or can be persuaded to do so, any more indeed than the United States can be persuaded to curb its overindulgence? The national energy policy unveiled by President Bush in February 1991 largely ignored recommendations from his own Energy Secretary to reduce the consumption of oil by cars and inefficient heating and lighting. However it did contain proposals to open up a wildlife refuge in Alaska to permit off-shore oil drilling and to expand the development of nuclear power. Such developments put into perspective the progressive initiatives of countries like Denmark, and the deep suspicions which are harboured throughout the less developed world that the outpourings from the rich nations on the need to change our energy habits are anything other than hollow rhetoric.

A measure of this critical debate is taken up more substantively in Chapter 8. Of course it is easy to take a critical perspective from the relative luxury of the armchair, far more of a challenge to seek out positive and practical solutions. In the remaining paragraphs of this chapter, therefore, our objective is to take a step backwards to consider the importance of some of the rhetoric, and to look at the potential for what we might call 'sustainable energy futures'.

The impact of the Brundtland Report

Domestic solar power on a house roof in Australia.

The Brundtland Report *Our Common Future*, produced by the United Nations World Commission on Environment and Development in 1987, has been referred to in previous chapters and is brought into sharper focus in Chapter 9 when we deal with the whole issue of international co-operation and sustainable development. One of its principal concerns was global energy, as the quote on the opening page of this chapter makes clear.

Clearly, what the Brundtland Report means by a 'low energy path' is very much akin to the targets for 2030 proposed by the Danish Alternative Energy Plan. What both the Report and the Danes appear to be saying is that energy efficiency can, in the short term at any rate, reconcile environmental concerns with economic development for all nations. It can effectively stretch energy supplies and literally buy time to develop alternative energy sources.

The Report sees a number of key elements of energy sustainability that have to be reconciled. Principal amongst these are the need for:

- sufficient growth of energy supplies to meet human needs 'for the foreseeable future' (which would mean accommodating a minimum of three per cent per capita income growth in the less developed countries)

- energy efficiency and conservation measures such that waste of primary resources is minimised

- priorities for public health, recognising the problems of risk to safety inherent in energy sources (particularly nuclear)

- protection of the biosphere and prevention of more localised forms of pollution, as well as controls on transboundary pollution that gives rise to such effects as acid rain.

In order to achieve this, the Brundtland Report requires a collective effort from both the more and less developed countries to use resources efficiently. Most urgently, it focuses on the continuing dilemma of the heavy reliance on fossil fuels and the increasing risk of global warming.

'No nation has the political mandate or the economic power to combat climate change alone. It is essential to develop, as soon as possible, internationally agreed policies for the reduction in emission of the "greenhouse gases", and the adoption of strategies needed to minimise damage, and to cope with the climatic changes and rising sea-level.'

Our Common Future, 1987.

The Brundtland Report also clearly asserts that progress can and should be made now in developing and extending the recent steady gains in energy efficiency, such as has been demonstrated in countries like Denmark, and shifting the mix more towards renewable sources. It documents the urgent need to reduce industrial air pollution and to restrict to an absolute minimum the damage it causes when it moves to other areas. A great deal of research has already been carried out in Scandinavia, for example, on increasing levels of acidity produced by acid rain, the most likely generating sources of which are the coal burning power stations of the United Kingdom.

'Reduction strategies [for acid rain] are certainly within reach and economic. Such strategies are a cheap insurance policy, compared with the vast amount of potential damage that they seek to avoid.'

Our Common Future, *1987.*

On the continuing unsolved problems of nuclear energy, the Report stresses the need for 'international co-operation and agreement' on a number of specific items including: the transboundary movement of all radioactive materials; internationally accepted standards for waste disposal; and the reporting of both routine and accidental discharges from nuclear installations. It adds, significantly, that 'The generation of nuclear power is only justifiable if there are solid solutions to the presently unsolved problems to which it gives rise'.

Amidst all the debate about 'technological solutions' the Report also tackles the critical issue of dwindling supplies of wood fuels in some of the least developed nations. In 1980 the Food and Agriculture Organisation estimated that some 1.3 billion people lived in 'wood deficit areas'. Continued overharvesting at 1990 rates could see a further one billion people living in such areas by 2000. These figures reveal great human hardship. Urgent strategies are needed to ensure both replanting and the more equitable distribution of fuelwood supplies. It is all too easy to forget in the 'energy indulgent' nations of the developed world that nearly half the world's population depends on wood as their main source of fuel. Greater understanding is required of the fundamental role that fuelwood plays in many local economies, and of the social relations governing its production and use.

▷ **Collecting fuelwood in Burkina Faso (formerly Upper Volta), West Africa.**

In summary, the Brundtland Report emphasises three interrelated objectives to achieve the goal of a low energy path globally:

- maintaining the momentum of energy efficiency
- ensuring 'effective' energy conservation measures
- realising the untapped potential of renewable energy.

Sustainable energy futures

This very brief insight into 'energy futures' in what has been called 'the most important document of the 1980s on the future of the world' shows some clear lines of parallel thinking with the Danish alternative plan, although Denmark was not a main contributor to the Brundtland Commission. The point is that the Report demands to be taken seriously. It is more than just hollow rhetoric. It has established a controversial political and economic agenda to take the planet towards the twenty-first century and has set up an important political process of international debate which is continuing. It also contains contradictions, but more of this later.

The message is a relatively straightforward one: the technology exists to enable sustainable energy futures to be achieved globally; but it will require some great acts of political will allied with enlightened economic thinking. Should we be optimistic that the rhetoric will be transformed into reality?

In terms of the opportunities for energy efficiency and conservation the Danes have shown the way for other developed nations to follow and clearly it is up to the developed world to take a lion's share of the

◀ **A freeway in Los Angeles, California.**

responsibility here. For example, we know that transportation across the globe already constitutes the largest and most rapidly growing drain on oil reserves and is also a major threat to the environment. Technically it is possible to extend car fuel economy beyond an average 65 miles per gallon and existing technology could increase new car fuel economy in the US from the current level of 22 mpg to 33 mpg at little extra cost to the consumer.

> 'If the price of gasoline were to increase in the US to reflect its full costs – economic, environmental and geopolitical – as it has in other nations, US consumers might demand more fuel-efficient cars and regulations for increased efficiency would make more sense.'
>
> *J.H. Gibbons* et al., *1989.*

After the oil crisis of 1973 the industrialised world made significant strides in improving energy efficiency, but it has since largely reverted to bad habits. The best way to encourage conservation and higher efficiency is for the world's leading nations to come to some agreement on a series of tax increases over a number of years, including a 'carbon tax' on fossil fuels. This would provide a cushion for investment for companies prepared to develop conservation strategies and/or alternative sources of energy. There are no hopeful signs from the US at the time of writing that this is going to happen soon in the place where it really matters.

There is increasing commitment towards renewable energy in many developed countries, with Scandinavia leading the way. There are also signs in the UK that interest in alternative energy is set to receive more attention, following the Gulf War and the privatisation of the electricity supply industry. The Government has signalled its intentions to increase considerably its commitment to funding research on how far existing, non-renewable fuels can be substituted and replaced by renewable sources like wind and wave power. Such a commitment is long overdue.

Of course, there are environmental side-effects to the development of such alternatives also, but there is no such thing as a 'simple energy choice'. They are all complex and all involve trade-offs of one form or another. The point is that some of the choices and the trade-offs are better than others in that they offer the scope for further development with less environmental damage. This is the essence of the concept of sustainability.

The developed nations have choices but do these choices extend to the less developed countries? To enable China, for example, to improve energy efficiency would require large transfers of technology and capital from the industrialised world. That country does not possess the resources to achieve it alone and certainly will not be 'told' what it can or cannot do. Clearly, we cannot underestimate the political dimension here. China is perhaps the

A hydro electric dam in Tanzania, funded by the World Bank.

biggest example, but it does illustrate the dilemma which confronts both the more developed and the less developed world. So here is a further test of political will.

'It is the collective response of developing countries to opportunities for efficient resource use in their economies that will determine humanity's ultimate success in slowing the deterioration of the global environment.'

J.H. Gibbons et al., 1989.

This may be so, but the burden of responsibility still rests with the industrially advanced nations to point the right direction and help less developed nations with sympathetic and creative programmes of investment and technology transfer. One of the ways they can do this is to agree an international convention on global warming that does not adversely affect the development opportunities for the poorer nations. That is the meat of the discussion to come.

CHAPTER 8

Atmospheric change: evidence and response

'Unfortunately, there was no direct equivalent for global warming of the dramatic discovery of the 'ozone hole' over the Antarctic. The fact that seven of the ten years in the 1980s were amongst the warmest since records began, and that there were unexpected droughts in the USA and severe storms around the world in 1988, lent warnings about global warming a popular credibility that they had previously lacked.'

Owen Greene, 1991.

In late 1990 the representatives of 137 countries met in Geneva at the Second World Climate Conference. Their agenda was apocalyptic: does the Earth face the prospect of significant warming as a result of an enhanced greenhouse effect and, if so, what should be done about it? These questions had already been answered for them by the Intergovernmental Panel on Climatic Change (IPCC), a team of over 500 scientists. IPCC reports had concluded that global warming over the next century would be about 4 °C, taking the world's temperature to levels unprecedented in recent geological history. They had also identified the overall reduction needed in emissions of the main greenhouse gases – carbon dioxide, CFCs and methane – making it clear that dramatic reductions were needed.

However, the politicians wanted more than global predictions and prescriptions. They wanted to know how global warming would affect their countries and they wanted an agreement which would allow them to pursue their economic development goals, ideally imposing the lion's share of any cuts on *other* countries. This raised two sets of difficulties. Scientists at present lack the ability to make detailed regional predictions, so faced some scepticism about their overall message. Politicians faced the problem of sharing out cuts between countries with a number of plausible principles available, each of which would benefit some and penalise others. Their response was to duck this issue by setting an overall target of stabilising greenhouse gas emissions at current levels but without agreeing how this should be done. Instead, they agreed on further investigation leading up to a further conference in Rio de Janeiro in 1992.

Why was their response so equivocal? In particular, why was it harder to agree a convention on global warming than it had been on ozone depletion? The ozone story has many parallels, scientific and political, with the global warming story.

Ozone depletion

Like greenhouse warming, ozone depletion was being discussed as a possibility by scientists well before it was taken seriously by politicians. Damage to the ozone layer was raised in the US in the early 1970s as an argument against building a large fleet of supersonic transport aeroplanes. The aeroplanes were never built and ozone depletion faded from public attention. But this early debate did identify the probable results of ozone depletion, that is, the increasing incidence of skin cancer. How would this occur?

Ozone is a blue gas with a pungent smell. It is a form of oxygen containing three atoms instead of the usual two. It is extremely toxic, even

◀ **Previous page**
Instruments flown from the British Antarctic survey station at Halley Bay first detected the 'ozone hole' in 1984.

in low concentrations, which makes it fortunate that it is rare (measured as a few parts per billion) and that 90 per cent of the ozone in the atmosphere is in the stratosphere, mainly between 20 and 35 km above the surface in what is known as the 'ozone layer'. Although it is diffuse even there, it plays an essential role in absorbing harmful ultraviolet radiation. It removes all the UV-C and much of the UV-B. In fact it is also *produced* by ultraviolet radiation, which causes ordinary oxygen to split into single oxygen atoms, each of which attaches itself to an oxygen molecule to form ozone. In recent years another source has been added: sunlight can produce ozone from industrial and vehicle pollution near the surface. Such ozone is itself a serious pollutant, contributing to forest damage, but stratospheric ozone is beneficial because it saves plants and animals on the surface from exposure to potentially harmful ultraviolet rays. It is estimated that a one per cent reduction in atmospheric ozone will increase the incidence of UV-B by two per cent and probably raise the incidence of skin cancer by two per cent. Given that skin cancer affects hundreds of thousands of people and kills about 12,000 people a year in the USA alone, a two per cent increase in skin cancers is a significant threat. As scientists also expect increased UV-B to lower the effectiveness of human immune systems, reduce photosynthesis in some crop plants, damage aquatic organisms and disrupt the atmosphere's heat balance by cooling the stratosphere, the threat of ozone depletion is a serious one. However, as long as the threat remained a theoretical one, little was done.

We are now so used to thinking of chlorofluorocarbons (CFCs) as the villains of the ozone story that it is hard to appreciate how improbable this once seemed. These compounds were adopted as refrigerants from the 1930s because they were stable, non-toxic and non-inflammable. Their cheapness and stability also made them ideal as aerosol propellants and for blowing bubbles into foamed plastics. It was first suggested in 1974 that this stability could allow CFCs to reach the stratosphere and interfere with the natural ozone balance. There was an intense debate in the USA which culminated in a ban on the use of CFCs in aerosols (then 75 per cent of releases) and a great reduction in emissions. However, no other country followed this lead and even in the USA ozone depletion ceased to be a concern. Neither the existing climatic models nor the 'Dobson network' of ozone monitoring stations gave any indication of any substantial depletion. Nevertheless, growing use of CFCs and continued scientific debate prompted the UN to organise the Vienna Convention of 1985 where 20 countries agreed that steps should be taken to protect the ozone layer.

A dramatic change in public perception of the ozone issue followed the revelation in early 1985 that the British Antarctic Survey research station at Halley Bay had detected a halving of ozone levels in their early spring,

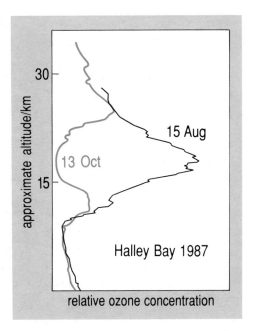

Figure 8.1 *Between mid-August and mid-October 1987 95 per cent of ozone between 14 and 23 km over Halley Bay was destroyed. This confirmed the observations first reported in 1985.*

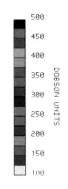

Computer enhanced map of the ozone column over the Southern Hemisphere on 3 October 1987 based on observations from NASA's Nimbus 7 satellite.

as shown in Figure 8.1. The image of the 'Antarctic ozone hole' was a major contributor to public concern, both because of the link to cancer and because the reality was suddenly seen to be much worse than any of the scientists had predicted.

Whereas previous investigation of ozone depletion was looking for a change of a few per cent in an already fluctuating concentration, the particular conditions in the Antarctic had produced a massive reduction. Indeed, it is said that NASA failed to detect the ozone hole because the data it received from satellites and aircraft were logged by a computer which had been programmed to discard observations which were outside the usual range of variation. So the significant new information was treated as error and ignored. However, once the Halley Bay results were known, NASA's formidable resources were brought to bear to confirm the size of the depletion and to identify the cause.

There were two reasons why the Antarctic spring was the occasion of massive depletions of ozone. First, the extreme cold of the Antarctic winter isolates the Antarctic atmosphere by creating the 'polar vortex', a belt of strong westerly winds in the stratosphere surrounding an area of high pressure. Second, in early spring the sun begins to reach parts of the atmosphere in which small particles of ice form polar stratospheric clouds. On the surface of these ice particles the chemicals that destroy ozone are

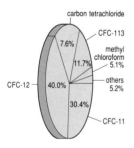

Figure 8.2 *Percentage contributions to ozone depletion by chlorine compounds of anthropogenic origin.*

produced in high concentrations. The identity of the key chemical was established by high altitude flights by NASA's ER-2 research aeroplane (formerly the U-2 spy plane). This showed a perfect match between high concentrations of chlorine monoxide (ClO) and low concentrations of ozone. The chlorine could be linked back to *chloro*fluorocarbons and solvents like chloroform and carbon tetrachloride. Rather small amounts of chlorine could create massive ozone damage because the chlorine works through a catalytic cycle (see the box).

Following the discovery of the Antarctic ozone hole and the broad agreement in Vienna that precautions were needed, it was soon established that CFCs were the principal causes of ozone depletion, as illustrated in Figure 8.2. It was also clear that, in spite of earlier controls in the USA, the atmospheric concentration of these substances was increasing steadily. In 1987 a meeting attended by 20 countries agreed the Montreal Protocol, which required a 50 per cent reduction of emissions of CFCs by 2000. This intergovernmental action was accompanied by pressure group campaigns, notably by Friends of the Earth, against the use of CFCs in aerosol sprays and massive public support persuaded manufacturers to phase out CFCs from spraycans very quickly. For a while, many people thought that the problem was solved.

DETERMINANTS OF OZONE CONCENTRATIONS

The amount of ozone present in the stratosphere is determined by three sets of processes:

- the balance between *creation* of ozone (by dissociation of oxygen by ultraviolet radiation and combination of oxygen atoms with oxygen molecules) and *destruction* of ozone (by dissociation of ozone molecules hit by ultraviolet radiation)

- further destruction of ozone by trace gases of natural origin, especially nitric oxide, methane and chloromethane

- more recently, additional destruction by gases derived from those produced by human technology, especially chlorine.

It is estimated that the current chlorine concentration in the atmosphere, i.e. three parts per billion, is five times higher than the natural level. CFCs are a particularly effective carrier of chlorine into the stratosphere because they are stable and insoluble in water. (Much larger quantities of methyl chloroform, a solvent and cleaning fluid, are vented to the atmosphere but most of it breaks down and the chlorine is washed back to the surface by rain.) In the stratosphere, even CFCs are broken up by ultraviolet radiation and hydrogen chloride and chlorine gas released. The chlorine can then destroy ozone molecules, as follows:

$$O_3 + Cl \rightarrow O_2 + ClO$$
(ozone plus chlorine becomes oxygen and chlorine monoxide)

$$O + ClO \rightarrow O_2 + Cl$$
(an oxygen atom plus chlorine monoxide becomes oxygen and chlorine)

The two step process (called a catalytic cycle) leaves chlorine gas ready to destroy more ozone – in fact each atom is estimated to be capable of destroying 100,000 molecules of ozone. The process also uses up free atoms of oxygen (O) which might otherwise have combined with molecules of oxygen (O_2) to create ozone (O_3).

Very similar catalytic cycles can occur with nitric oxide, hydrogen and bromine (derived from halon fire extinguishers) in place of chlorine. Indeed, chemists now believe that well over 100 chemical processes influence ozone concentrations, many of them linked by feedback relationships. This makes exact prediction difficult. However, the very long lifetime of CFCs in the atmosphere and of chlorine in the stratosphere, together with the protracted operation of catalytic cycles, means that ozone destruction will continue for decades even if new releases of ozone destroying gases are phased out quickly.

It soon became clear that the problem was not solved and that there were major problems yet to be overcome. First, only weeks after the Protocol had been agreed, NASA scientists published the results of a two year study which concluded that ozone reductions of five per cent or more had occurred, particularly in the southern continents and the mid-latitudes of the northern hemisphere. These reductions were larger than those predicted by atmospheric models, suggesting that the processes of ozone destruction had not been fully explained. Second, it was soon realised that, because of the rapid increase of emissions in the 1980s and the amounts of CFCs already in the atmosphere, even a 50 per cent reduction in emissions would lead to continued growth in chlorine concentrations, as shown in curve A of Figure 8.3. Third, while use of CFCs in aerosols was easily phased out, there was a case for increased use in refrigeration equipment in less developed countries. This raised a political issue: 80 per cent of CFC consumption and almost all production were in the more developed countries, which were clearly responsible for ozone depletion. Yet blanket reductions would penalise poor countries where more refrigerators were urgently needed.

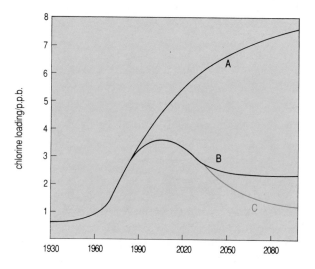

Figure 8.3 *Projections of future chlorine loadings of the atmosphere for different control strategies : A original and B revised (1990) Montreal Protocol (both with 50 per cent substitution of CFC market by HCFCs; C total cessation of all anthropogenic emissions of chlorine compounds in 2030.*

The Montreal Protocol included provisions for review and in fact negotiations proceeded urgently in 1989 and culminated in London in 1990. This new agreement covered many more countries and laid down that CFCs, halons and carbon tetrachloride should be phased out by 2000 and methyl chloroform by 2005. Because of the cost implications of using more expensive substitutes in refrigerators, less developed countries – led by China and India – refused to sign until a multilateral fund was set up (with a budget of $240 million for the first three years) to assist transfer of technology to them. This was agreed, the first time that more developed countries had accepted explicit responsibility for the problem and the need for support from the less developed countries in solving it.Unfortunately, contributors to this fund have been slow in coming forward and in mid-1991 only about $10 million had been deposited.

In practice this rapid phasing out of CFCs means that chemical companies will have to substitute hydrochlorofluorocarbons (HCFCs). These are related compounds, already in limited use, with much lower ozone depletion potential. However, they do contain chlorine, so some will reach the stratosphere and damage will continue. It is predicted that this will follow curve B in the figure. HCFCs are regarded by the amended protocol as 'transitional substances', to be replaced in due course, probably by hydrofluorocarbons (HFCs) which contain no chlorine. Only then is there a prospect of a significant reduction of chlorine concentrations (curve C). However, both HCFCs and HFCs are yet to be fully evaluated and they could have other disadvantages. In particular, they may, like the CFCs, be powerful greenhouse gases and hence contribute to global warming.

Global warming: the problem

The stories of global warming and ozone depletion are similar in many ways: both are concerned with changes to the behaviour of the atmosphere as a result of changes in trace gases concentrations; both were anticipated by scientists well before they were taken seriously by governments and industry; both are difficult to detect in practice and both involve international disputes as well as scientific debate. However, there is one crucial difference: ozone depletion is caused by a set of rather rare substances which can potentially be replaced with other less harmful substances. Global warming, on the contrary, is caused by gases which are the inevitable outcome of some of the most central activities of industrialised societies. Because of this, global warming is the ultimate pollution issue, bringing together natural and social processes and symbolising the urgent need to review society's use of and impacts upon natural systems.

The science of the greenhouse effect was introduced in Chapter 1, where it was pointed out that it plays a vital part in raising average surface temperatures from well below freezing to 'just right'. So the problem is the possibility of a greenhouse effect enhanced by society's emissions of waste gases and perhaps behaving in dangerous new ways. Indeed, the rise in temperature is not in itself particularly problematic. What does cause alarm is predictions of substantial rises in sea level, changes in weather patterns leaving some areas drier than at present and a higher frequency of extreme events like gales and floods. But first we need to look at the evidence.

Like ozone depletion, global warming was identified as a likely problem long before there was any evidence. Indeed, the evidence remains inconclusive. Climatologists now agree that there has been a rise in temperature of about 0.5 °C since 1860, as shown in Figure 8.4. However, it is evident even from this figure that temperature fluctuates a great deal over time as well as space. Although measurements are confined to the last few centuries, it is clear from indirect evidence – from written records of events like rivers freezing, from pollen analysis and from the species of fossils in rocks – that some past periods have been considerably hotter and others colder than the climates of today. The coldest glacial periods were about 3 °C colder than today and the warmest interglacials about 1 °C warmer. So the evidence shows an upward trend in a fluctuating phenomenon. Two more steps are needed to show why global warming is a matter of such concern.

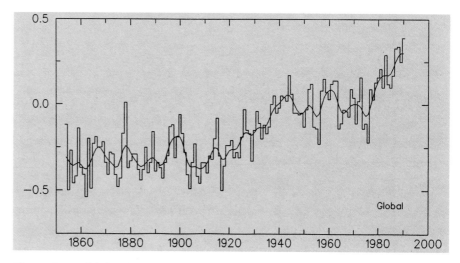

Figure 8.4 *Global average temperatures from 1860 to 1990, plotted as deviations from the mean. The smooth curve is the mean of successive five year periods.*

The first step is to identify a likely causal mechanism and to show that the causal factors are themselves likely to grow. The prime cause, as identified by the Swedish scientist Arrhenius in 1896, is the increasing concentration of carbon dioxide in the atmosphere – principally as a result of burning fossil fuels. As described in Chapter 1, carbon dioxide absorbs long wave radiation coming from the Earth's surface and heats the atmosphere. There is evidence that carbon dioxide concentrations are related to atmospheric temperatures: analysis of air trapped in ice sheets shows that carbon dioxide content rose from 190 p.p.m. to 280 p.p.m. as glacial periods were replaced by interglacial periods. Historic data, as shown in Figure 8.5, were at about 280 p.p.m. in 1800 and rose steadily through the Industrial Revolution and at an ever more rapid rate in the twentieth century. The 1988 level, 350 p.p.m., is 10 per cent greater than that of 1958 and, unless preventive action is taken, future levels will continue to rise rapidly. To make matters worse, the warming effects of carbon dioxide have been supplemented by other greenhouse gases: methane concentration has doubled since the Industrial Revolution and CFCs are extremely powerful greenhouse gases with no natural precursor. The rapid rise in greenhouse gases suggests an increasingly rapid rise in atmospheric temperatures and the prospect of exceeding the highest levels in recent geological history, with the rate of temperature increase one hundred times faster than ever before.

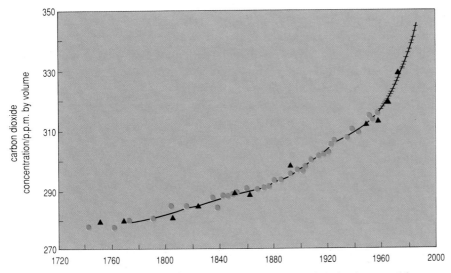

Figure 8.5 *Increase in the atmospheric concentration of carbon dioxide, determined from ice core measurements at Siple station Antarctica (triangles), isotope analysis (circles) and direct observation at Mauna Loa (crosses).*

At this point, the second stage in the argument is reached: what will be the effect of the rise in greenhouse gas concentrations on temperatures and on climatic patterns? This ceases to be a matter of evidence and requires the use of scientific models (see the box on page 139). Most analyses have focused on the likely effects of a doubling of carbon dioxide levels above the pre-industrial level. The estimates fall into the range 3–6 °C with 4 °C the most probable figure. Such a rise would take global temperatures well above any level which has occurred in the last few million years. How soon might it occur?

To put a time-scale on this change, it is necessary to predict the likely change in emissions of carbon dioxide and the other greenhouse gases. That takes us out of the realm of science and into economic forecasting – an even more difficult enterprise. Figure 8.6 shows the contribution to global warming attributed to different gases and Figure 8.7 shows the contribution of different activities. It is clear that the main contributor is carbon dioxide released from the burning of fossil fuels, but growing problems are carbon dioxide released by deforestation, methane from agriculture and natural gas leaks, nitrous oxide in vehicle exhausts and CFCs. The growth in emissions has been spectacular: world energy use quadrupled between 1950 and 1984 and carbon dioxide emissions tripled in the same period. The future prospect is for even more rapid growth unless action is taken. The link between emissions and atmospheric concentrations is mysterious: about half the carbon dioxide emitted disappears from the atmosphere but scientists cannot at present identify where it goes. Without this fortunate accident, the predictions would be even more alarming. As it is, the worst case estimate (in other words, the fastest likely rate of emissions) would double carbon dioxide by 2040, the most probable case would delay doubling until the end of the century. Only the most optimistic assumptions about control of emissions yield any hope that the doubling can be prevented. However, that takes us on to the question of political response and there remains a crucial step in understanding the problem – the effect of a rising temperature on other things, notably on sea level, the frequency of extreme events and on ecosystems.

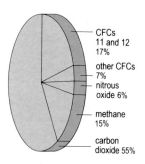

Figure 8.6 *Estimated contribution of each greenhouse gas to global warming in the 1980s.*

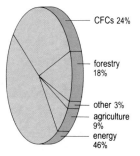

Figure 8.7 *Estimated contribution of different human activities to global warming in the 1980s.*

ATMOSPHERIC MODELS

Most people are aware that engineers designing a car or an aeroplane can build a scale model and test its aerodynamic properties in a wind tunnel. But many people watch TV weather forecasts without realising that future weather patterns are predicted using another sort of model. Scientific study of climate and weather, together with the laws of physics, has enabled meteorologists to construct models consisting of sets of equations linking temperature, pressure, wind, humidity and other variables to each other and tracing the effects from place to place. The equations can be solved by a computer over different time periods to give forecasts of what will happen in the future. However, no one in Britain would deny that forecasting the weather is very difficult.

Predicting future changes in the Earth's climate is also difficult, though the broad scale of analysis does make it easier by making it unnecessary to trace detailed changes like the ones which plague British forecasters. However, at a global scale the atmosphere is affected by the oceans, the ice sheets and the continents, and the time-scale is very long.

Current models, called general circulation models (GCMs), are limited by the available computer power and divide the Earth's surface into no more than a few thousand cells, solving the equations for July and December conditions. There are several different GCMs operational, using somewhat different approaches and equations. They all give the same broad predictions but disagree about the likely outcomes for particular areas.

These models have been tested in a number of ways: predicting short-term seasonal changes, predicting the detailed pattern of energy losses to space, 'predicting' past changes to climate as a result of the known rise in carbon dioxide and even 'predicting' the development of the climates of Mars and Venus. These tests have given climatologists a general confidence in the models, but revealed some inadequacies, notably that predictions of past warming due to carbon dioxide are double those actually observed. As a result, a great deal of work is going on to develop better models.

The effects on sea level are once again difficult to calculate since they involve measuring past changes in a variable which fluctuates over time and between places, some of which are well recorded but many of which are not. The best current estimate is that between 1910 and 1980 average sea level rose by 9 cm, a rate of 13 cm per century. This broadly coincided with the rise in global temperature, but estimates of both values are uncertain so the rate of change might be as little as 10 cm per 1 °C or as much as 40 cm per 1°C. Indeed, things become even more uncertain when the effects of rising temperatures on ice sheets are considered. The melting of mountain glaciers is reasonably predictable, but the effects on Greenland and Antarctic ice sheets less so (the former may shrink but the latter may grow). Most uncertain of all are the effects on the West Antarctic ice shelf: at worst this

▲ *The Antarctic ice sheet is the largest reservoir of water outside the oceans.*

▶ *The relatively thin coastal ice shelves around Antarctica could be broken up by global warming.*

Coral atolls, like this one in the Maldives, would be disastrously affected by a small rise in sea level.

could become unstable and huge quantities of ice fall into the sea. At present it is thought unlikely but it has the potential of raising sea level by several metres – more than all other factors combined. All these predictions are complicated by the huge mass and slow response time of oceans and ice sheets: rises in atmospheric temperatures will take a very long time to raise the temperatures of ice and oceans. All in all, predictions of sea level rises are very speculative, with the IPCC report suggesting a range from 3–10 cm per decade, but this is of little comfort to countries like the Maldives, whose highest land is 2.5 metres above current sea level, or Bangladesh, where flooding of coastal lowlands is already frequent and disastrous.

Shandib Island, Bangladesh. The cyclone of November 1970 caused terrible loss of life.

The effects on extreme events are also difficult to predict. The mechanism which would cause them is, however, clear: hotter sea surfaces would mean more evaporation and more heating of the atmosphere. In certain crucial zones, notably between latitudes 8° and 15 °N and S of the equator, heating and evaporation already trigger occasional cyclones. These are intense low pressure areas with winds up to 200 kph and torrential rain storms. When they reach the land they can do immense damage. At worst, when the low pressure and high winds cause coastal floods, the damage can be appalling. The cyclone of 12 November 1970 killed some 300,000 people in Bangladesh, and was the worst storm since 1727. Only 21 years later, the storm of 30 April 1991 had comparable effects. Global warming could increase both the frequency and the energy of such events – and also of mid-latitude gales and storm surges like the ones which affect the UK. Because such events occur sporadically, it is hard to know whether recent extreme events such as the hurricane force winds which struck southern England twice in three years are just part of a long established pattern or are really the harbingers of a new phase in which extreme events are more common.

The effects on ecosystems and on agricultural crops will depend not only on higher temperatures and more frequent events like frosts and gales but also on the direct effects of carbon dioxide enrichment on rates of photosynthesis, and hence plant growth. As a result, some plants may grow faster but others will be eliminated by frost or gale. To make detailed predictions, one would need to know how temperature and rainfall would change in each area, but current GCMs are not reliable at such a local scale. Indeed, they often disagree markedly in their local predictions of rainfall, in many cases differing over whether it would become wetter or drier.

Even from this brief sketch it must be apparent that predictions of the extent and effects of global warming are extremely difficult. But because the causal mechanism is clearly identified and the rapid growth in greenhouse gas concentrations is probable, the large majority of scientists agree that global warming will happen. In some ways the uncertainty about the rate of warming and the local effects may be politically beneficial: all countries are equally threatened by unpredictable change. If some countries could be confident that they would benefit – with higher temperature and rainfall bringing agricultural prosperity to new areas – it might be even more difficult to negotiate a concerted international response than is already the case.

Responses to global warming

The threat of global warming has been taken increasingly seriously, first by scientists and later by politicians, over the last 15 years. It was one of the topics of discussion at the First World Climate Conference in 1979 and became a concern of international bodies like the UN Environmental Programme (UNEP) and the World Meteorological Office (WMO). A major step forward, both in scientific understanding and public awareness, came with the publication in 1986 of the 29th report of the Scientific Committee on Problems of the Environment (SCOPE 29). This report made the first authoritative prediction that doubling of carbon dioxide concentrations would raise global temperatures by 3–6 °C. It also pointed out that

◀ *Hurricane Gilbert caused extensive damage in the Caribbean and, shown here, Texas in 1988.*

emissions of carbon dioxide could quadruple in the next century if preventive action was not taken. Following SCOPE 29, a further international conference was convened in Toronto in 1988, attended by representatives of 48 states. 1988 was an extremely hot year over much of the globe and a number of extreme events occurred. Accordingly, the conference agreed that a 20 per cent reduction of carbon dioxide emissions was needed by 2005. However, no attempt was made to formalise an agreement and more research was commissioned from IPCC.

The IPCC findings were the major input to the Second World Climate Conference in Geneva in 1990. Three areas were covered: predictions of extent and impacts (where the SCOPE 29 analyses were broadly confirmed but developed in much greater detail) and possible responses. The authors argued that the problem could not be reduced by any known 'technical fix', that relying on the ability of natural and social systems to adapt was extremely risky in view of the magnitude of the changes in prospect, and that the optimum response was to prevent the problem from arising. Prevention was agreed in principle by the conference but the stated goal was to stabilise *emissions* of greenhouse gases while ensuring sustainable development of the world economy. Such stabilisation was shown by the IPCC analyses to imply continued growth in *amounts* of greenhouse gases in the atmosphere and hence continued global warming. Why had such a modest goal been set – indeed one which was markedly less ambitious than the 20 per cent reduction in emissions agreed in Toronto two years earlier?

An obvious contributory factor was that three times as many countries were represented in Geneva as in Toronto and so the views of the less developed countries were much more strongly advanced. They may well have been encouraged by the success of India and China in demanding financial support for signing the Montreal Protocol on CFC reduction. The less developed countries were able to demolish the case for a simple across-the-board percentage reduction of greenhouse gases. They were responsible for only 15 per cent of all past emissions and only 30 per cent of current ones, in spite of containing about three-quarters of the world's population. They therefore argued that the problem had been caused by the industrialised world, which should therefore bear the brunt of any reductions. Within the industrialised world, Western countries were quick to point out that the USSR and East Germany had very high emissions even though their GNPs per capita were not all that high. Similarly, Japan and Europe were critical of the high emissions of the USA. Many countries were critical of Brazil's high emissions because they resulted as much from burning the Amazon forest as from rapid industrialisation. More detailed analyses showed a substantial variation in emissions per head among the more and less developed countries as well as between them.

Given this complexity, the Second World Climate Conference kept to very broad principles: stabilisation was needed but should be carried out in an equitable way. Further investigation and negotiation would take place before the 1992 Rio de Janeiro conference on environment and development. Meanwhile, flexibility also became a principle, as commercial organisations, nations and groups of nations were encouraged to take appropriate action. Japan, Canada, Australia, New Zealand and the EC made unilateral commitments to stabilise or reduce greenhouse gas emissions by the end of the century, but the USA and USSR remained sceptical and many of the less developed countries continued to demand the right to expand energy use in the future. In this complex situation, what kind of actions would be appropriate?

Two principles combine to indicate the kind of changes that would be appropriate. First, the areas where emission controls should be concentrated are the areas with the biggest impact on global warming. Second, given the uncertainties which bedevil prediction of the effects of global warming, it makes sense to concentrate early preventive action on issues where there are other good environmental reasons for action. Fortunately, these two principles seem to be consistent with each other and to direct attention to the following four policy areas:

Energy use This is the biggest single source of greenhouse gases, contributing nearly half of all emissions. Without policy change, the amount of carbon dioxide emitted could triple by 2025. Three-quarters of present impacts come from the effects of carbon dioxide but methane is produced in incomplete combustion and leaked from natural reservoirs. Trace gases, like nitrous oxide and ozone, are emitted by vehicle exhausts or produced by the action of sunlight on exhaust fumes. So a range of local pollution problems, together with the problem of sustaining supplies of oil in the future, combine with global warming to indicate the need for policy change on energy use. The kind of policies which are needed are those described in Chapter 7: firstly, energy efficiency – using machines and buildings which are better designed and constructed to achieve the same results with less fuel input (a particular form of energy efficiency is reusing waste heat for space heating, notably in combined heat and power schemes); secondly, using new sources of energy supply, especially renewable technologies to generate electricity and substitute vehicle fuels like ethanol or methanol. All these changes have been shown to be technically feasible and some of them would begin to generate savings after a very few years. The task for governments is to phase out subsidies which encourage the inefficient use of energy and create cost and tax incentives, possibly including carbon taxes, to encourage adoption of energy efficient technology.

CFCs These are such powerful greenhouse gases that they are already responsible for 24 per cent of additional warming. Moreover, they have such long lives in the atmosphere that it is certain that they will continue to contribute their effect for a century or more. Fortunately, their elimination has already been agreed as a result of the Montreal Protocol. However, it remains vital that CFCs are not replaced with substitutes which are also greenhouse gases. The HCFCs appear more promising because of their shorter lives but are not yet fully investigated in terms of impacts on global warming.

Deforestation Especially in the tropics, this contributes 18 per cent of current greenhouse gas emissions. The causes were outlined in Chapter 3 and include clearance of land for agriculture, exploitative forestry and use of wood for fuel. The first two make no economic sense, as well as being environmentally harmful, and the third can be reduced by growing more trees for fuel and by using better stoves or alternative fuels. The problem is that it is the governments of developing countries who are nearest to this issue and they may be unconvinced that forest should be preserved and/or powerless to resist logging companies or large landholders. Existing international collaboration needs to be developed and made more effective.

Agriculture In addition to its energy use and its pressure on forests, agriculture contributes nine per cent of greenhouse gas emissions. Two main gases contribute: methane is produced by livestock and by rice paddies while nitrous oxide is given off by land which has been fertilised with nitrogenous materials, whether organic or inorganic. Any sharp reduction in these emissions is improbable: rice paddies are vital to feeding vast Asian populations and livestock can hardly be fitted with methane tents. Fertiliser use seems certain to rise in developing countries even if it can be limited elsewhere. Some limited contributions could be made: agricultural waste could be fed into methane digesters which would supply a fuel to substitute for oil or natural gas as well as preventing methane escaping from slurry reservoirs. Similar treatment could prevent methane escapes from domestic rubbish tips, as could incineration of rubbish.

Conclusion

It is clear that atmospheric change is both a formidably complex problem for scientific understanding and a major challenge for international collaboration. Although uncertainty remains, both ozone depletion and global warming pose significant threats. In both cases, prevention is the best remedy and the international community has made a serious start to secure agreements which will at least limit the speed at which things get worse. In devising policies to tackle these global problems, it is fortunate that the main policy changes which are needed are consistent with the changes needed to solve many other environmental problems. Some of the policy changes will actually save money in the short to medium term which can be used to tackle more costly problems. There is no reason to suppose that the problems are insoluble.

However, it is already clear from negotiations over ozone depletion and at the Second World Climate Conference that international agreements are made much more difficult by the unevenness of development. The more developed countries, which have created most of the changes in the atmosphere, seem to reap most of the benefits. The less developed countries have the major goal of providing better living standards for their huge populations through rapid development. But it is now clear that if they follow the same development path as the more developed countries it will threaten catastrophic change to the climate. An alternative form of development is urgently needed. That is the concern of the next chapter.

CHAPTER 9

Towards a sustainable future

'It is both futile and indeed an insult to the poor to tell them they must live in poverty to protect the environment.'
Gro Harlem Brundtland.

'We must think globally but act locally.'

Gro Harlem Brundtland, May 1990.

We ended the last chapter by referring to the need for, and the difficulty in obtaining, international agreement on global warming, and suggested that what is urgently required is some alternative form of development that is far less damaging to the environment. The trouble is that while many of the world's most urgent environmental problems are now widely acknowledged, like the greenhouse effect, deforestation and pollution from the inefficient and wasteful use of energy, we are by no means united in solving them.

The first international environment conference took place in Stockholm in 1972 and established a benchmark for political action by which subsequent international meetings were to be judged. In the same year, a controversial publication entitled *Limits to Growth* carried this foreword from the then UN Secretary General, U Thant:

'I do not wish to seem overdramatic, but I can only conclude from the information that is available to me as Secretary General that the members of the United Nations have perhaps 10 years left in which to subordinate their ancient quarrels and launch a *global partnership* to curb the arms race, to improve the human environment, to defuse the population explosion, and to supply the required momentum to development efforts.'

Limits to Growth was rejected by the technocrats of the industrialised world as being doom-laden and without proper scientific foundation, but it did focus attention on global resource issues and helped to raise environmental awareness. Twenty years on, U Thant's prognostications have something of a prophetic feel to them that serves to strengthen the underlying message of the political rhetoric. Since 1972, millions of words have been spoken and written about the need to control global development and safeguard the environment, but how much nearer are we to achieving realistic international co-operation on issues of global environmental concern? Mounting global problems show us that we face a crisis in decision-making, nationally and internationally. Is it feasible to talk in terms of international co-operation on the environment when individual governments, particularly, though not exclusively, in the industrially advanced countries, are yet to be held to account for clearing up the mess in their own backyards?

In this chapter we examine how the international community in the 1990s is responding to the challenge laid down by the United Nations two decades earlier. It is to UN inspired initiatives that we turn our particular attention, specifically the World Commission on Environment and Development (UNCED) which began sitting in 1983, chaired by Gro Harlem

◁ **Previous page**
Street scene in an Indian town.

Brundtland, sometime Prime Minister of Norway. The Commission reported in 1987, and is continuing its round of international deliberations.

The focus of the Report, *Our Common Future*, is *sustainable development*, a concept that has been referred to on a number of occasions in previous chapters. Here we take a more in-depth and critical look at the term. What exactly does it mean, who is likely to benefit from it, and whose responsibility is it to actually achieve it? Does sustainable development offer the human race signs of hope in using and managing the Earth's resources and relating to one another? Or is it, as some cynical observers would have it, merely the latest in a series of political bandwagons wheeled out by the richest nations to protect what they already have, and to dictate to others less fortunate how they should use their limited resources? The relationship between the less developed and the more developed world will be a crucial factor if a sustainable future is to be secured for all the world's people.

A global agenda for change

In drawing up its 'global agenda for change' the Brundtland Commission called upon the full participation of 22 nations[*], 13 of which were from the less developed world, and received contributions from a host of others. In this vital respect, the final report could not be criticised for taking a 'developed world' perspective, even if the initiative largely owed its inspiration to the industrialised countries. This global representation, in what has become known as the Brundtland Process, is continuing up to what is being widely regarded as a 'watershed' international conference, Eco '92, in Brazil in 1992. Important stages along the way have included regional conferences in Bergen (May, 1990) and New Delhi (September, 1990), to which references are made later.

Essentially, the original terms of reference drawn up by the United Nations in 1983 are those which underpin this whole process of international debate. In summary they are: to propose long-term environmental

▶ *Gro Harlem Brundtland addressing the Eco '92 Public Forum in New Delhi in September 1990. With her on the platform are several representatives from both the more developed and less developed world.*

[*] The 22 participating nations were: Algeria, Brazil, Canada, China, Colombia, Germany, Guyana, Hungary, India, Indonesia, Italy, Ivory Coast, Japan, Mexico, Nigeria, Norway, Saudi Arabia, Sudan, USA, USSR, Yugoslavia, Zimbabwe.

strategies for achieving sustainable development by the year 2000, and to recommend ways concern for the environment may be translated into greater co-operation among developing countries and between countries at different stages of economic and social development, leading to the achievement of common and mutually supportive objectives that take account of the interrelationships between people, resources, environment and development.

At a conference organised by the International Institute for Economic Development (IIED) in London in March 1991, HRH The Prince of Wales made the following remarks:

> 'It is at the community level that most is being done to protect the environment. We can all too easily get caught up in global negotiations whilst forgetting that people need to be free to pursue sustainable development for themselves. The reconciliation of environmental protection with economic advance essentially comes down to a mass of local problems. These all add up to global issues, but the solutions are local. Providing the right conditions for solutions at the local level is the challenge for governments.'

The Prince's statement mirrors the quote at the beginning of this chapter, and establishes a meaningful political criterion by which to assess the potential for achieving sustainable development. But we must first examine the concept itself.

Sustainable development: an achievable goal?

There is nothing new in the concept of *sustainability* as such; it is the political and economic context that is of paramount importance. It is in this respect that the idea of sustainable development has been received as being innovatory and as challenging conventional wisdom. The Brundtland Report first adopted the term and gave it serious definition. Since then definitions have proliferated, leading many critics to surmise that here was merely the latest political buzz word to emerge from the industrialised world in its attempt to display genuine concern for the global environment.

This is what Gro Harlem Brundtland had to say about the concept in Bergen in May, 1990:

> 'The mandate that the United Nations General Assembly gave for a new commission focusing on the environment was coupled with population pressure, with the differences between rich and

poor, the need for technological transfer, the way we tackle all these issues as one entity, because they are all linked together. That was the kind of mandate which was really, you know, nearly an impossible kind of mandate to give anyone to address. On the other hand, we had to start addressing it as a holistic idea, and then we found the words "sustainable development" to cover best the combination of environment and development, the links between economy, ecology, and between poverty and environment.'

Bergen, 1990 (in a BBC/OU televised interview).

The Brundtland Report defines sustainable development as: 'Development that meets the needs of the present without compromising the ability of future generations to meet their own needs. It contains within it two key concepts:

- The concept of needs, in particular the essential needs of the world's poor, to which overriding priority should be given.

- The idea of limitations imposed by the state of technology and future needs.'

This definition contains at least four serious implications:

1   Concern for the relationship between resource use, population growth and technological development.

2   Concern for the production and distribution of resources of food, energy and industry amongst the more developed and less developed nations of the world.

3   Concern for 'uneven development' and 'underdevelopment', for the gross imbalances between rich and poor nations, for equity.

4   Concern for environmental degradation and potential ecological disaster.

Overall, the Brundtland concept of sustainable development focuses concern on human need rather than human want.

In stressing *need* and in focusing on *world poverty* and *development* issues, the Brundtland Report provides clear evidence for the connections between poverty and environment in less developed countries, and acknowledges the essential linkages between the more and less developed world that involve critical economic and strategic issues.

In emphasising need, the Brundtland Report appears to be offering a fundamental challenge to the materialist and consumerist values of the industrially advanced nations; but is it equally challenging the industrialising aspirations of many developing countries? Is it offering a challenge to industrialisation, to *industrialism* as such, or only to industrialism in certain 'unacceptable' forms? For instance, what is the ethical or moral position of those in environmental movements in the more developed nations who are saying to the less developed countries that they are forbidden the benefits of an industrialised society lest they further pollute the planet? For them, Gro Harlem Brundtland has an unequivocal answer, as we stressed in Chapter 5: 'It is both futile and indeed an insult to the poor to tell them that they must remain in poverty to protect the environment.'

This statement implicitly poses some fundamental questions about what we mean by progress and development, and how we measure them. It also raises the even more awkward issue of the descent into even worse poverty if the environment is *not* protected. To what extent is economic growth an adequate measure of development anyway, if by development we mean the relatively crude indicators of increasing Gross Domestic Product (GDP) or Gross National Product (GNP), neither of which takes any account whatsoever of environmental costs? Such indices derive from the capitalist model of economic development, with its emphasis on profit and free market principles. For many in the less developed countries, this is a model of economic dependency with its persistent and dominating overtones of colonialism and imperialism.

There is certainly a conviction running through the Brundtland Report that the free market principles that effectively govern international economic relations would be inappropriate and prejudicial to the interests of better environmental management in the less developed nations. It explicitly recognises that change can only be achieved as a result of political action over the environment, which is clearly a highly controversial and contested area. But how can such change be brought about? We need to probe the analysis further.

The Report sees the issue of environment and development in terms of a series of *interlocking crises*: an environment crisis, a development crisis, an energy crisis. We have already looked at some of the essential elements of these in the previous chapters: *population growth* – UN estimates as to when the world population will 'stabilise' vary between 8 billion and 14 billion sometime next century, with less developed countries accounting for over 90 per cent of the increase from the present figure of over 5 billion; *economic activity and technological improvement* – industrial production globally has grown more than 50 times during the present century, and four-fifths of this growth has occurred since the end of World War II in an increasingly inequitable manner; the *resources gap* between the more developed and the less developed world is widening, and it is the industrialised nations that have exploited the greater part of the Earth's natural resources, its *ecological capital*.

This inequality is the world's main *environmental* problem; it is also its main *development* problem. One of the major features of inequality is that while new technology, the mainspring of economic growth and development, might offer alternatives or options in terms of the more efficient use of resources, and in particular in the use of renewable resources as we saw in Chapter 7, the industries that are now the most 'resource hungry' and potentially the most polluting are those growing in less developed countries; but it is precisely here that there is both more urgency for growth and less capacity to minimise damaging side-effects. A case study of Thailand later in the chapter aptly illustrates this point. At the same time, there are no guarantees for the more developed world that new technology will not bring with it more harmful side-effects!

Making it all happen!

Land erosion in Burkina Faso, West Africa.

The boxes on the next page give a summary of the Brundtland Report's broad recommendations. Essentially, sustainable development is seen as a *total concept*, as a desirable policy objective arising out of a positive but critical analysis of development processes. It is a prescriptive approach, providing an agenda, although not necessarily a blueprint, for action, the responsibility for which is placed firmly in the hands of governments, agencies and individuals. Responsibility might equally be placed in the hands of the big multinational companies or transnational corporations (TNCs). It emphasises the 'absolute priority' for a global, international response, allied with 'essential institutional and legal changes'. At the same time, it also stresses the crucial importance of local, community-based initiatives, and repeatedly underlines that a primary goal is 'greater equity', both among and within nations.

As will be apparent from the boxes, the Report deals very much in generalisations rather than with specific technical issues. Sustainable development is seen as a process for harmonising resource use, investment, technological development and institutional change. In short, it is projected as a 'grand design' for global action and change. Is this what a group of 'mainstream' politicians really believe should and can happen? It may only be an agenda, but the political implications are for turning the world economic order on its head. It is difficult to imagine the fundamental changes that will be necessary in governments and societies (as prescribed in the second box), but these concerns remain centre stage in terms of international debate, so we must continue to run with them!

Brundtland's 'strategic imperatives'

1 Reviving growth
Sustainable development must address the issue of poverty, because poverty increases pressure on the environment.

2 Changing the quality of growth
This means making 'growth' less materialistic, less energy intensive and more equitable in its impact.

3 Meeting essential human needs
This is especially important in terms of food, energy, basic housing, fresh water and health.

4 Ensuring sustainable population levels
The challenge is to tackle the highest rates of population growth, especially in Africa. But it is also a challenge to the more developed world, for this is not just about numbers, but also about rates of resource consumption.

5 Conserving and enhancing the resource base
This involves a moral argument (the notion of good stewardship) as well as an economic one. It includes agricultural resources, forestry, fisheries and energy.

6 Reorienting technology and managing risk
The capacity for innovation needs to be greatly enhanced in developing countries, and technological development generally must pay greater attention to environmental factors.

7 Merging environment and economics in decision-making
Economics and ecology should not be seen in opposition but as interlocking, in effect treated as a single science.

Brundtland's 'institutional imperatives'

1 A **political system** that secures effective citizen participation in decision-making.

2 An **economic system** that is able to generate surpluses and technical knowledge on a self-reliant and sustained basis.

3 A **social system** that provides solutions for the tensions arising from disharmonious development.

4 A **production system** that respects the obligation to preserve the ecological base for development.

5 A **technological system** that can search continuously for new solutions.

6 An **international system** that fosters sustainable patterns of trade and finance.

7 An **administrative system** that is flexible and has the capacity for self-correction.

Refrigerators being mass produced at the large Kelvinator plant near New Delhi, India.

The entire credibility of the Report hinges on the premise that major economic growth can be achieved in ways that sustain and even enhance environmental capital. Development, Brundtland emphasises, is the best way of achieving population control, and growing populations in the developing world should be sustained at economic levels 'above the minimum' to satisfy fundamental need, because improvement of the quality of life is a basic tenet of the whole thesis. This means an increase in consumption patterns for many countries, but this cannot occur in the materialist mode of the industrially advanced nations. So, in effect what the Report is saying is that development for the less developed nations has to be different from that experienced in the past, and the more developed countries have got to change their consumerist habits!

A critical questioning of the findings raises a whole series of issues: are economic growth and development synonymous concepts? Can sustainable development really be concerned with meeting human needs, maintaining economic growth and conserving resources all at the same time? Does 'sustainable development' mean all things to all people? There are clearly many value positions and assumptions underlying the concept.

A rolling programme: from Bergen to New Delhi

It is easy to criticise the Brundtland Report: it is optimistic, over-ambitious and too far-reaching. Moreover, it has been seen by its critics, especially in the less developed world, as a conscience-salving exercise for the rich nations. Yet the process of discussion, debate and participation, set in motion back in 1983, continues on an ever-broadening front, and surely this is the crucial point: the impact that the process is having on 'consciousness raising' amongst governments and the public at large across the globe. 'We must have talk as a prelude to action,' comments Maurice Strong, the United Nations Secretary who chaired the Stockholm Conference and who is chairing the 1992 conference in Brazil. The message coming back from the non-governmental organisations (NGOs) and the youth groups at the Bergen conference, both of which were well represented, was: 'Words, more words, but still no action! When is the talking going to end and the action begin?'

At Bergen, the 34 member nations of the Organisation for Economic Co-operation and Development (OECD), effectively the industrially advanced nations, produced many more words, and the rhetoric was once again about producing a 'joint agenda for action'. Gro Brundtland restated the underlying theme of the UN Commission:

'The Earth is one, but the world is not [...] There will be no sustainable development in the world if this takes place only in the north. There can be no sustainable development as long as poverty is a scourge from which more than one billion people suffer.'

She came closer to aligning with some of the Commission's critics when she qualified the interpretation of 'growth' in the Report:

'We need a stronger sense of environmental responsibility both in public policies and planning, and in corporate boardrooms. Long-term sustainability has yet to reach the same importance as short-term profitability as a measuring rod for corporate success. Business must be profitable to survive, but it must also face the call to become sustainable to enable us all to survive.'

Bergen, 1990 (in a BBC/OU televised interview).

This sense of 'corporate responsibility' was taken on board but given a more radical flavour in an alternative agenda, drafted by delegates from non-governmental organisations. This argued that to achieve genuine sustainability there must be 'profound changes in the world's economic and power structures, as well as parallel changes in domestic power structures in both the North [more developed countries] and the South [less developed countries]'. Such changes have to be based upon the principles of equity, participation and accountability, with specific attention given to the needs and rights of those who are presently marginalised in society: women, the poor, the landless, and indigenous or tribal peoples.

The alternative agenda continues:

'In order to eliminate the economic discrimination against the south, northern countries must give high priority to changing lifestyles in their own societies in order to become real models for sustainable development. There must be a reversal of flow of wealth in the form of debt repayments from the south to the north. Stability of commodity prices must be ensured, together with fair access for these commodities to international markets.

Rich northern countries should recognise a responsibility and commitment to provide substantial resources and compensation to developing countries. They should take actions which are for the common environmental good and global security, and which involve the foregoing of immediate economic benefits.'

Non-governmental organisations, *An Agenda for Action*, 1990.

In two crisp paragraphs this gets to the nub of what achieving sustainable development really means. In all of this discussion we cannot ignore the perspective from the less developed countries. Many observers from the less developed world continue to argue that the industrially advanced nations have an immense historical debt to pay. The consequences of following the conventional path of economic development over 200 years of history have been disabling and dependency-creating for much of the developing world. These are manifest in rising debt, in structural adjustment programmes, and in trade protectionist policies.

Yet, equally, developing countries have a responsibility. In Chapter 5 we referred to the comments of Maneka Gandhi, the Indian Junior Environment Minister (1990-1991): 'Of course it's our responsibility. What we say is that it is the fault of the West, but there's a difference between fault and the responsibility of each country to do their bit towards putting it right. It's just that we say we'd like some help from you, technologically and financially.' (New Delhi, 1990.) It is the responsibility of countries like India, destined to have a population of around one billion by 2000, to develop in a manner that will ensure more than a minimum standard of living for all its people, whilst at the same time safeguarding the environment as far as possible. Yet, as we saw in Chapter 3, huge projects like the Narmada Valley scheme, largely financed by international capital, are having considerable environmental impact, and are not necessarily benefiting the local people either.

International 'help' in this form is not what Maneka Gandhi, a long-time opponent of the Narmada project, means. She favours local schemes that fully involve local people. Participation was a major theme in the New Delhi conference in September 1990 and much debate focused on what realistic choices countries in the less developed world have, when confronted with an international economic order that clearly works in the interests of the richest nations. A number of delegates argued strongly that millions of people in developing countries like India are having to confront the contradictions of 'development' merely to survive.

What the Delhi conference did highlight was the breadth of awareness of concern about the links between environment and development, and the willingness to get involved in the whole debate about sustainability. 'Development' can take many forms. Dr Rachendara Pachauri, Director of the Tata Energy Research Institute in New Delhi, makes an important point about development and energy policy:

'We have no choice but to increase energy consumption, but we don't necessarily have to follow the same path that was followed by the rest. It is essential to increase energy production and given

The Tata Energy Research Institute 'Energy Bus' arriving at the Kelvinator plant near New Delhi to undertake an energy audit.

the choices that we have, the technologies that are available, they'll have to be a mix of big projects and small projects. What we need to accelerate right now is to develop grassroots capabilities for implementing small-scale projects, and several of them are viable.'

New Delhi, 1990 (in a BBC/OU televised interview).

We look at one such local initiative below and follow this with an assessment of achieving sustainable development in Thailand, which has one of the fastest growing economies in the world.

Sustainable futures: two examples

A sustainable energy project in Haryana State, to the north-west of New Delhi, was initiated on an experimental basis in 1984 by the Tata Energy Research Institute (TERI), an organisation that is mostly funded by the Tata Industrial Group, one of the largest corporations in India. The aim has been to demonstrate the practical achievements of work in the field on local renewable sources of energy. The project has centred on one village, Dhanawas, which has about 300 inhabitants, with the long-term objective of spreading the ideas to other villages in the state.

Participation by the villagers is a cornerstone of the initiative, in what is clearly a 'bottom-up' process. All work has been undertaken in complete co-operation with the village council, with the concept of the common property resource (a concept that we met in Chapter 3) as a lynchpin of resource management and use policies. There has been to date (1991) no costs borne by the inhabitants, funding coming jointly from TERI, the Indian Government and the Food and Agriculture Organisation (FAO).

The principal features of the project have been:

- The establishment of an 18 acre plantation on what were very poor saline soils supporting only scrub vegetation. The policy is for long-term improvement of soil quality, using hardy nitrogen-fixing species like acacia and mesquat which can be used as a source of much needed fuelwood on a sustainable basis. All the trees are held as a common property resource.

- The development of a number of biogas makers, which use a mixture of cow dung and water. The capacity of each unit is two cubic metres per day, which is sufficient for about five hours cooking on modern cookstoves or 10 hours of lighting. The plan is to introduce enough units to make the village self-sufficient in renewable sources of fuel, reducing the consumption of fuelwood in conventional cookstoves.

- The building of a gasifier, which uses a mixture of shredded mustard stalks, cow dung and water in the form of small pellets and converts them into gas. The equipment is capable of generating the equivalent of five kilowatts of electricity with an 80/20 gas/diesel mix – enough power to provide lighting for the whole village.

- The use of solar powered water heaters.

Essentially, the project concerns the use of intermediate technology to promote the efficient use of renewables, thus cutting the cost of provision for conventional fuel consumption in rural areas. It is not being suggested that such projects can solve the problems of energy use in the cities. A central problem is that Haryana State is amongst the most agriculturally productive states in India, and the inhabitants of Dhanawas have been willing and able to participate because their village is relatively rich. Poorer villages have other priorities, like access to safe water and income genera-tion. Nevertheless, the TERI project does demonstrate what can be achieved locally with a small budget and political co-operation. Here are the influen-tial views of Dr Anwel Khotari, a leading Indian environmentalist:

> 'It is only through an aggregation of people's power where people reside, where you can have an effective dialogue with those who are in power today. It is only this aggregation that can help in a process where people come in to their own, where they begin to have a vested interest in the regeneration and recovery, and the health of the resources on which they live. It's only when there is that feeling of partnership with nature, when you are able to

▲ Feeding a mixture
of cow dung and water
into a biogas maker,
Dhanawas, Haryana
State, India.

◄ Feeding mustard
stalks into a shredder
attached to a gasifier,
Dhanawas, Haryana
State, India.

spread the ethic of *walking softly on the Earth*, that you would be able to have genuine development in a long-term sense, not short-term development maximising production, maximising profits and then distribution.'

New Delhi, 1990 (in a BBC/OU televised interview).

Nevertheless, such local initiatives are taking place within a context of continuing pressure for economic growth nationally, as the Narmada project illustrates. In India, it is a question of striving to achieve a balance between huge, national multi-million dollar projects and small-scale local schemes, with the emphasis not necessarily on the former.

In Chapter 5, we examined how Thailand's phenomenal rate of economic growth is causing major environmental problems in the capital, Bangkok. Thailand has achieved such remarkable sustained growth because of a consistent record of macro-economic stability and an enduring commitment to undertake structural economic reforms. This is a carefully worded reference to the influence which the World Bank, in particular, has had in contributing to structural reform programmes in Asia. It needs to be emphasised that the substantial input of foreign capital, including aid, to boost development in Thailand is certainly creating wealth, but a significant proportion goes abroad again in the form of export capital, especially on debt repayments and as profits to the transnational corporations.

The paradox is that such economic dynamism co-exists with severe economic, social and environmental problems. For although economic

▶ *A new kindergarten, located in the heart of Klong Toey, the largest slum in Bangkok, Thailand.*

growth has undoubtedly been a primary factor in the reduced incidence of poverty, continuing high rates of population increase, coupled with a severe imbalance in terms of distribution (a feature of continuing patterns of rural–urban migration), have applied relentless pressure on natural resources and on an inadequate infrastructure.

Is sustainable development an achievable goal in Thailand, or is growth being achieved at a price? Despite the industrial expansion, Thailand is still a heavily resource dependent country, with natural resources continuing to make an important contribution to GDP. Even so the share (by value) of agricultural products in Thailand's exports fell from 48 per cent in 1981 to 34 per cent in 1986, while the share of manufactured products increased from 35 to 55 per cent over the same period.

There is certainly a recognition by a concerned minority in Thailand of the need for policies directed towards sustainability and conservation. Equally there is an uneasy acceptance that many economic development projects have paid too little attention to the long-term sustainability of their natural resource base. The extent of the structural transformation of the Thai economy from an agricultural and resource-based producer and exporter to a more modern and industrial-based economy is, for some critical observers, a manifestation of the fundamental contradictions inherent in the concept of sustainable development.

To concerned Thais, however, the official response is that growth is essential as the only solution to poverty, and that increased awareness of

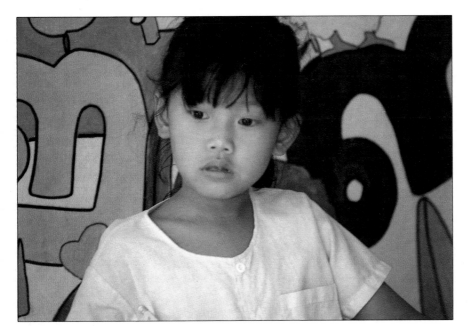

◀ *A sign of hope for the future? This little Thai girl in the Klong Toey kindergarten is drawing a picture of how she sees her world.*

environmental issues will ensure that Thailand will not make the same mistakes as the industrialised nations. One particular safeguard being stressed is the incorporation of 'state of the art' technologies into the forefront of the development process, supported by loans and the transfer of technology from the West.

'Despite its acknowledged problems', argues Dr Dhira Phantumvanit, one of the country's foremost environmentalists, 'Thailand has a real opportunity to pioneer in an emerging field of sustainable development. Much of the groundwork has been laid, even though the legal and administrative framework cannot yet exploit the full potential of the investments already made' (1987). There is certainly a sense amongst leading politicians and economists that Thailand can 'contain growth' and steer a course towards sustainability.

There is a powerful argument that economic growth and industrialisation are essential to eradicate poverty in the developing world – this is a cornerstone of the Brundtland Report. However, the free market-based approach embraced by Thailand through her strong structural ties with the more developed countries of the West is hardly likely to produce an equitable distribution of resources internally, and the price being paid in environmental terms is considerable. We can make a similar argument in relation to India, particularly regarding development projects like the Narmada Valley programme.

Conclusion

We have tried to cover a lot of ground in this chapter and inevitably have skimmed over a number of issues that are complex and clearly beyond the scope of this current text. Hopefully, we have given a certain insight into the Brundtland Process, which is of great importance in terms of the future of this planet. At the same time, our aim has been to highlight some of the contradictions which are apparent in the concept of sustainable development. The two case studies have attempted to show, in different ways, the challenges that face developing nations in striking some sort of balance between the need and the demand to industrialise, in the face of increasing pressures, especially from the international community, to safeguard the environment, where choices are often heavily constrained.

What is apparent is that responsibility for achieving sustainable development is a global one, resting both with the more developed and the less developed nations, if not in equal measure. Yet perhaps the maxim of thinking globally but acting locally is an apt one. The positive approach in

Dhanawas emphasises the significance of participation and bottom-up initiatives, so that it may be wholly appropriate to assert that sustainable development is ultimately a local activity. After all, it is not governments that carry out the development, but people. However, is 'local' a realistic overriding context for tackling environmental problems that are truly global? Is there political and economic realism here? For instance, have not national aspirations and goals to be seen in a far wider, global context, and have not habits of production and consumption in the industrially advanced nations, like the UK, got to change sooner rather than later? It is to these questions that we turn in the final chapter.

CHAPTER 10

'Think globally, act locally'

'Compared with private cars, all forms of public transport are
vastly more energy efficient and vastly less destructive to the
environment.'

John Seymour and Herbert Girardet, 1987.

'The Earth is one but the world is not. These words express how closely we share our most urgent problems – yet we have not united in solving them. We must act now, *under the signs of impatience and hope*, to reverse the escalating threats to our global environment. We have only a very short time to design and implement the necessary changes in our attitudes and policies. The changes we make – or fail to make – will have a decisive influence on the survival of life on Earth.'

These are the words of the Norwegian Prime Minister and former Chair of UNCED, Gro Harlem Brundtland, in forthright mood at the Bergen Conference 'Action for a Common Future' in May 1990. We began this book in equally forthright mood by arguing that 'we should use our undoubted ingenuity to change society to coexist more harmoniously with natural systems' (Chapter 1, page 17), rather than face the unacceptable (so far as the human race is concerned) alternative futures posited: the Gaia hypothesis that 'the planet can eliminate human society and revert to a golden age of natural systems in harmony', and the more probable hypothesis that there will be a future in which human society is left 'with reduced access to degraded natural systems, and possibly with falling quality of life and life expectancy' (Chapter 1, page 17).

It is this latter scenario that Gro Brundtland and the Commission on Environment and Development set out to confront in *Our Common Future* (1987), in its sequel *Signs of Hope* (1990), and in the whole process of international deliberation and debate leading up to the World Conference, organised by the United Nations, Eco '92, in Rio de Janeiro in June 1992. We have examined in some detail the central theme of this process – sustainable development – particularly in the previous chapter, but we are inevitably left with questions about the 'how', the 'who' and the 'when' of sustainable development, and 'in whose interest?'.

This is symptomatic of our own and others' reservations regarding the concept and the practicalities of achieving it. Yet, one of our initial objectives in setting out to write a book about global environment issues in the 1990s that was both accessible and relevant, was to avoid being overly pessimistic, and indeed, quite the opposite, to promote debate about what could be done in a positive sense. That is not to say that we have refrained from taking a critical stance, where it seemed appropriate, or have pulled any of our punches, although there will be those who will probably argue that we could and should have punched a good deal harder. And of course that is their prerogative.

It is all too easy to be critical when the view from the window is over the green and wooded countryside of the North Downs of Kent, relatively untouched as yet by a second motorway ring for London, or urban sprawl,

◁ **Previous page**
A tram in the centre of Innsbruck, Austria.
The tram is the safest and cleanest form of
mass urban transport.

or, so far as the senses are able to tell, highly damaging pollutants. That situation is partly a matter of personal preference but mainly one of privilege. Were this to have been written by citizens of a less developed country, say in one of the slums of Mexico City or Bangkok, then clearly quite a different emphasis and point of view might emerge. This may seem like stating the obvious; but although we can lay claim to the benefit of being able to take a 'global perspective', we do live in an industrialised society, the first to become so, and we inevitably take on board the values and attitudes of that society.

As we said in the last chapter, many critical observers from the less developed world are very sceptical about the role of the industrially advanced nations in establishing policy guidelines for dealing with major global environmental problems. The West for them has been the traditional developer, coloniser and exploiter. They see the role of science and technology not as liberator but as destroyer. They point to the huge annual expenditure on armaments, a continuing growth industry that for them epitomises the worst face of free market capitalist enterprise.

> 'Modern technology has made it possible to deliver a bomb across the world in minutes. Women in rural areas in Asia and Africa still walk several hours a day for the family's water supply.'
>
> *The Quaker Movement, 1989.*

At the same time, economic growth and exploitative development are taking place in many less developed countries, as we have seen, for example, in the rain forests of Brazil and in a rapidly industrialising Thailand; and the Brundtland Report is demanding that we cannot expect poor countries to remain in poverty in order to protect the environment. So, what to make of it all? We have to accept a number of fairly basic points: that development (value-laden term that it is) is essential for all nations and particularly the less developed; that economic development is not the same as economic growth (as defined in advanced capitalist societies in terms of GNP and GDP, both of which exclude any reference to environmental costs); that sustainable development concerns particular forms of economic activity that minimise environmental damage and actually enhance environmental 'capital', in relation to the careful management of resources; and that *all* the blame for the current mess that has been made of this planet cannot be laid at the door of the more developed countries, culpable though they undoubtedly are.

That list surely leaves out some important issues, but it is enough to be going on with. The main problem for most of us is how to make sense of all this in terms of the 'environment' as we experience it, in our own local surroundings. We may be concerned, but how far can we take effective action at a local or national level, let alone at a global level? We have posed a lot of questions about the feasibility of achieving sustainable development, so perhaps we should attempt to provide at least some answers.

We ended the last chapter by endorsing, with qualifications, the maxim: 'Think globally, act locally'. Acting locally is certainly a very significant key in the process, but isolated or unco-ordinated examples of individual or community-based action will not unlock the secrets of sustainable development globally. What we have been stressing throughout this book is the importance of recognising the interconnectedness of social, economic, political and environmental change at all levels – local, regional and global. Local action must be seen in the context of a continuous process of adaption and change across nations rich and poor. That being said, let us start in our own backyard.

Acting locally

Lloyd Timberlake of the International Institute of Environment and Development in London, speaking at a conference in 1990, stated:

> 'If we talk and write about environmental problems, we mislead ourselves, and we mislead our readers and listeners into thinking that there is some sort of environmental solution, some technical, scientific answer which can be put in place without involving us. If we can make clear that we are talking about economic problems, political problems, then it is quite obvious that everyone must be involved in the debate and in the solution.'

This line of thinking clearly underlies the theme of sustainable development. What is required is a change in attitudes and values about how we see 'progress' and how we assess and measure 'quality of life'. That is a first step. Environmental issues do not exist in isolation from economic, political and social processes and they certainly cannot be tackled in isolation. So is this is a matter for politicians, industrialists and scientists, and is what we do as individuals of any consequence?

The sheer scale of problems like global warming and pollution of the seas can indeed be daunting, but individual actions taken locally can have an impact, in a marginal sense, on the environment itself and more importantly on the attitudes of others. In recent years a number of publications have emerged dealing with the practicalities of taking 'environmental action' locally. Their general theme has been to stress 'green thinking', good housekeeping and practical economics. Some have stood out, notably *Blueprint for a Green Planet* by John Seymour and Herbert Girardet.

▲ **Urban motorway traffic in London, UK.**

One of Seymour and Girardet's arguments is to reduce, as far as possible, the use of 'essential' items like the car. Just how possible is it to leave the car at home, and 'let the train take the strain' for example? In Chapter 7 we referred to the possibilities of improving fuel economy in cars in the United States, where petrol costs about half as much as it does in Britain. Raising fuel costs via increased taxation may have the potential for discouraging the ubiquitous use of the motor car, but that is not particularly beneficial as a policy *in isolation* to reduce damage.

What would bring together enlightened individuals, interest groups (see Figure 10.1) and national government in Britain on a united platform to reduce the environmental damage caused by the car would be a co-ordinated and integrated transport policy, something that has yet to be formulated here. Within such a policy, two modes of public transport could play a leading role, as they have done traditionally: the train and the tram.

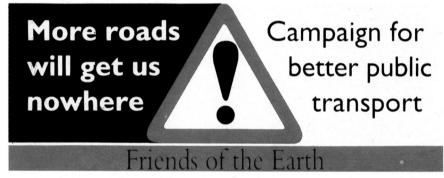

Figure 10.1 *1991 sticker from Friends of the Earth's continuing campaign, started in 1975. The British Government plans to spend £17 billion on roads in the next 10 years. British Rail needs £6 billion over the next four years to make their services work.*

In May 1991, the Conservative Minister of Transport, Malcolm Rifkind, announced plans for 'radical changes' in British transport policy, with a specific emphasis on a transference of freight movements from road to rail, stressing concern for the environment as a primary factor. Three months earlier, in February, the Department of Transport had published a lengthy report outlining the Government's spending for transport to 1994. Amongst its objectives were increased efficiency and conservation of the environment. Well over one-quarter of the report was devoted exclusively to roads, with a little over 10 per cent to the railways. While the word 'environment' appeared frequently in the text, there was no attempt to frame the proposals within an overall environmental policy context. We await developments with interest and a modicum of scepticism.

'Let the train take the strain' – British Rail, hopefully on time!

Arguably, a more considered perspective has been provided by the Transport and Environment Studies group (TEST), which spent five years preparing an in-depth study of the relative environmental effects of road and rail transport in Britain. Entitled *Wrong Side of the Tracks*, it tackled head on the thorny issue of the 'freedom' of the motor car, because it is private, individual, and appears free from state subsidies or intervention in the market. 'Privacy is gained at the expense of those needing public transport', TEST argued. 'Freedom to do what? To pollute others' ears and lungs, kill and maim them, obliterate much of what all transport users revere in the quality of urban and rural environments?'

Whilst it resorted to somewhat emotive language, the TEST study provided a considerable amount of statistical evidence to support its case that rail is safer, quieter and environmentally less damaging than road transport. Rail is by no means 'perfect' (what form of mass transport system is?) but it does lend itself to adaptation in its different forms to produce and sustain a better environment. Despite the arguments used by TEST and other transport groups, for rail to be given priority over roads will require a considerable shift in government opinion, not to mention the influence of the powerful lobby which exists to ensure that road transport retains its 'pride of place'.

A different form of rail transport is making a come-back to help combat traffic paralysis in our cities – the tram, albeit in revolutionary guise. Since the early 1980s, 45 urban rapid transit schemes have been put forward. The majority of these will be lucky to see the light of day, hampered by a mixture of political infighting locally and central government demands, ideologically determined, for private funding and the need to make a profit.

With a change of political heart (or perhaps party?), the desirability, in social and environmental terms, for accommodating a long-term public need for cheap, efficient above-ground public transport in Britain's most congested urban areas may yet be realised. What is required is a progressive programme of centrally subsidised schemes. In continental Europe every capital city except Paris has a tram network, and transport planners have been quick to capitalise on existing systems, with computerised systems which give priority over all other vehicles at junctions leading the way.

Amongst British cities, Manchester and Sheffield are in the vanguard, with, respectively, the £130 million Metrolink and £230 million Supertram schemes due to become fully operational by the mid-1990s. Tramways are far less environmentally damaging than any other form of vehicular transport in cities. They are economical to operate, fast, safe and, above all, clean. They are relatively cheap to build, energy efficient, and electric powering minimises the risks of pollution.

Of course, the generation of electricity itself, through the burning of fossil fuels, particularly coal, can have a major impact on the environment, as we discussed in Chapter 7. There are alternatives, in the form of renewable sources of energy, and the technology exists to improve the technical performance of existing power generating systems. All come at a price and also present the green lobby with a number of paradoxes.

For instance, the British Wind Energy Association claims that land-based wind turbine sites could meet one-sixth of UK electricity generation at current demand levels. Of course, windmill farms on the scale required would have a major visual impact on the landscape, and some environmental campaigners would not like that. The electricity company PowerGen wants to extend the quarrying of limestone within the National Parks in its processes to cut acid rain emission from power stations. The immediate result may be a government ban on extended quarrying in the Parks, but this will simply shift the environmental impact elsewhere.

Darlton quarry in the Peak District, Derbyshire, UK.

We appear to have ranged far and wide in this brief look at local action, but everything is connected. Much can be achieved by environmentally aware individuals, literally in their own backyards; much more if and when individual action is backed up by policy initiatives from central and local government, supported by powerful interest groups, particularly in industry and commerce, whose primary objective is not always to maximise short-term profits. Even so, whatever measures are taken, whether they be in the field of transport or energy policy, and given significant shifts in attitudes and value positions, there will always be environmental implications. There are no 'simple' choices to be made and there have to be trade-offs. Those which offer less environmental damage whilst sustaining development have to be preferred.

Thinking globally

Such attitudinal and value shifts are equally important in the international arena. If nation states in the more developed world adopt progressive development policies which have environmental impact at the centre rather than at the periphery of the decision-making process, then they will at least be setting an example for the rest of the world. Countries like Norway, Sweden and Denmark are at the forefront in this respect, but these do not, unfortunately, rank amongst the industrial giants of the more developed world.

As we hope the preceding chapters have shown, environmental issues become increasingly complex as we progress from a local to a global perspective. It is one thing to write about changes that could be achieved at home, quite another to postulate what might happen on the international stage. Chapter 8 referred to the difficulties in obtaining even basic international agreement on the need to curb the emission of greenhouse gases in relation to global warming. Those international conventions that are already in place, such as the Law of the Sea, are exceedingly difficult to enforce.

Yet the importance of international co-operation on global environmental issues, and the need for developing conventions or *regimes*, cannot be emphasised enough. This is a central tenet of the Brundtland Report. But co-operation has to go further. It is not about imposing our Western values on the poorer, less developed nations in some sort of post-imperialist neo-colonial manner. Maneka Gandhi asserted at the Oxford Union in February 1991 that poverty in India led directly from British colonisation, which had fostered a short-term view of land use. 'The economies of former colonies are still being manipulated', she declared. 'The only difference is that the mechanisms are now more subtle. Developing countries are now being manipulated by the trading system. Aid has its place in development, but the quality of aid is what counts.'

Professor Keith Griffin, former Master of Magdalen College, Oxford and Chair of Economics at the University of California, takes up this argument:

> 'The moral case for the people of rich countries to help those in poor countries remains intact. The prosperous have a moral obligation to assist those who live in poverty, and there is a prima-facie case for a transfer of resources from rich countries to poor. It does not follow, however, that there is a moral obligation to support official aid programmes.'

'Towards a humane way of giving', The Guardian 22 February 1991.

There is clearly a 'moral imperative' underpinning the concept of sustainable development, which comes through forcefully in much of the Brundtland discussions. Reinforcing the links between poverty and environmental degradation in the poorer countries, Sir Sonny Ramphal, the former Secretary General of the Commonwealth, and President of the

World Conservation Union, gave this warning at the IIED Conference in London in March, 1991:

'Unless the developed world is willing to do more to alleviate the plight of developing countries, many of them will hardly be able to move beyond their hand-to-mouth existence, let alone reach the point where they can provide for long-term sustainable development.'

At the same conference, the President of the World Bank, Barber Conable, expressed agreement with such an appraisal:

'Development and environmental protection are mutually dependent [...] Good economic policy is good environmental policy [...] As a development agency whose mission is to reduce poverty and improve social conditions, the World Bank, therefore, must also be an environmental agency.'

This appears to be a laudable statement, but beyond the consensual rhetoric of the international conference lies the reality of continuing deprivation and degradation in many less developed countries; and so-called 'development aid' has often exacerbated the situation. In June 1991 the US Congress threatened to withhold 25 per cent of America's 1992 contribution to the World Bank until it was satisfied about the Bank's

◀ *Tribal war dance to declare militancy against the Sardar Sarowar Dam, Narmada Valley project, Gujarat, India.*

serious intentions to implement environmental reforms. The message from Congress was that although the Bank is seen to be making some progress here, many projects, and particularly those in India and West Africa, are still doing huge damage and do not match up to the rhetoric! See page 180.)

Maneka Gandhi refers to the need for 'quality aid', but the general rule is for selfish conditions to be attached by donors, normally in the form of 'structural adjustment programmes', that is, 'you do it the way we tell you, or you don't get the money'. In India, huge dams, as in the Narmada Valley project discussed in Chapter 3, are being built for prestige purposes, explains Mrs Gandhi. On the other side of the coin, aid is frequently misused or abused by the recipient countries, either through naivety or, worse, corrupt practices.

Not all aid is misappropriated or comes with long strings attached, of course. There are numerous examples of projects, particularly those implemented at a smaller more local scale, which make a genuine attempt to link development and environment for a sustainable future. The village scheme in India cited in Chapter 9 is one such example. Thinking globally can be about acting locally, but in a global context.

However, as we stressed in the last chapter, acting locally is not sufficient for problems which are global in nature. Arresting the advance of desertification, for example in Africa, where food shortage will continue to be a major issue to be faced by the international community (as we saw in Chapter 4), will require increased co-operation and appropriate development aid for projects large and small. Even that may not be enough to help some countries like the Sudan, where political instability allied with a deep-seated (and partly understandable) mistrust of the West can nullify even the best intentions.

Mistrust is rooted in history, and is fuelled rather than dampened by contemporary international political and economic relations. What of the 'new world order' being heralded so triumphantly by President George Bush at the start of the decade? The format of this present text has not allowed for discussion of the environment and development problems being faced in the former countries of the Eastern bloc, though it is increasingly likely that they will be tackled within rather than outside the framework provided by market economics. The newly constituted European Bank for Reconstruction and Development has these issues high on its agenda.

What does this tell us about a new order? What will be *new* about it? To what extent will the Group of Seven (G7) – the world's seven leading industrial nations – play a lesser role in orchestrating international economic relations (for example, through GATT and the Organisation for Economic Co-operation and Development, OECD), during the 1990s than they have done throughout the 1980s? It is to be hoped that internal

The Group of Seven Heads of State at the London Summit, July 1991.

tensions amongst the seven (USA, Canada and Britain are all in economic recession, France and Italy are on the edge of it, whilst Japan and Germany continue to 'enjoy' economic growth) do not relegate debates about world poverty, debt and the global environment to the bottom of the political agenda, where they have tarried for too long. The following box tells its own story.

The need for commitment

The United Nations Environment Programme (UNEP) is being severely hampered in its attempts to curb global warming, in particular, due to a lack of funds. In 1990, the 'league table' of national voluntary contributions read as follows:

United States	$11.5 million
Japan	$6.8 million
Britain	$5.7 million
Germany	$5 million
France	$1.7 million
Spain	$590,000

Rest of Europe even less, with Italy not on the list at all!

Yet the global challenge is their challenge. Traditional ways of measuring growth that continue to exclude environmental costs have to be replaced by an economics that is sensitive to the environment. Environment and economics have to go together in decision-making, as the Brundtland Report demanded. But the most pressing environment and development problem is the accumulated debt of the less developed nations. In mid-1991 it had already exceeded $1 trillion, and since 1984 the interest paid to the rich countries has been greater than the flow of aid to the poorer countries, a situation which is simply absurd. There is no easy answer but signs of greater efforts by the Group of Seven to tackle the issue would be a step in the right direction.

The United Nations Commission on Environment and Development has come up with proposals, but ultimately it can only offer advice. To follow UNCED's guidance in terms of representation would provide an even bigger step. If G7 is indicative of the West at its most arrogant and imperialist, should it not be reformed and reorganised to include representatives from the less developed world? Perhaps that really would be the beginning of a new world order, but on whose shoulders rests the responsibility to initiate

▼ *Maurice Strong, prior to his speech to the UNCED Conference at Bergen, Norway, in May 1990.*

the reforming process? This could clearly be a case of 'physician heal thyself'.

Certainly, Maurice Strong, the present Chairman of UNCED (who also presided over the first environment conference in Stockholm in 1972), speaking in Bergen in May 1990 and looking ahead to Eco '92, is unequivocal about how we should be viewing the relationship between the richer and the poorer nations, and where the principal responsibilities for action lie:

> 'There is no way in which we can say to the developing countries: please don't grow, you might threaten our way of life, our growth. In the process of growing we recognise that we've endangered all of life on this planet, but now it's your growing populations and your desire to improve your economic life that seem to threaten us. That just won't fly. We can't expect them to freeze growth at current levels, freezing existing patterns of inequity and injustice in the world, freezing them at levels of poverty which are, you know, completely repugnant to any system of values to which we give service. We simply can't ask them to do that. They're just at the first stages of their growth and development. They need it, they have a right to it and they have a right to say to us: you can't stop our development. We need your help, and if you're going to ask us to move to a more sustainable way of development, you've got to help us do it.'

Prescribing the future

We may have left you with more questions than answers, but that is perhaps inevitable in a field of debate where there can be no easy answers. Yet we hope that we have provided some interesting and challenging responses to the major questions that this book set out to tackle: the importance of the environmental damage that is occurring globally, the principal reasons for this occurrence, and what could or should be done about it. In so doing, we have sought to emphasise the interconnections amongst a whole range of environmental problems, from a local to a global level, and we have shown how it is important to examine these problems in terms of both the physical and social processes involved.

It has not been our intention to provide some sort of agenda, green or otherwise, for future action over the environment. In this sense we are not attempting to prescribe the future. We have tried to assess the consequences of certain courses of action, particularly within the context of the Brundtland concept of sustainable development, but hopefully have avoided, as far as possible, ideological traps, political dogma or extreme viewpoints. That is not to say that we necessarily favour moderation as a virtue in the pursuit of everything; but we did set out to keep our feet on the ground and not indulge in flights of political or economic fantasy.

The problems are enormous but there is also a powerful ground swell of radical thinking and action, in both a local and a global context. For many, like the environmental and youth groups at the Bergen Conference, there has not been enough action; but there is continuing encouragement in the work of pressure groups, as we have stressed in earlier chapters, to arouse public opinion and activate politicians. Here again, the words of Maurice Strong:

> 'There's no question that there's still lots of words, and more words than ever; but words hopefully are a prelude to action. When politicians begin to pay lip-service to an issue, their constituents have a basis for making them accountable. So words tend to provide the basis for action and there has been a good deal of action since 1972. Not enough, of course, and therefore I welcome the words because it's our job to translate those words into action.'
>
> *Bergen, 1990 (in a BBC/OU televised interview).*

There is a measure of optimism in Maurice Strong's statements that does provide hope for the more immediate future, as UN inspired debate continues on an ever-broadening front globally, and the World Conference in Brazil in 1992 offers the prospect of providing a focus for sustained action. This would be a cautiously positive point at which to conclude our current exploration of the issues. Yet, whilst it is convenient, it is also very general and permits too much latitude within the political rhetoric.

Here are the comments of Wanagri Maathai, a member of the Kenyan 'Green Belt' movement, also in Bergen:

> 'You cannot just say you're going to prevent desertification or deforestation, just like that. It is not a single issue, it is not a single answer; it's a complex concoction of all kinds of issues that interplay and interlock. And when we try to solve these problems they're not going to be solved at the meetings, by the politicians, by writing beautiful documents. In the final analysis, the problems will be solved by taking action at wherever we are individually. That is why I would like to emphasise this concept of acting locally, but thinking globally. In the final analysis, each of us must make that decision to take action; but all the talking, all the documents go on. It has been going on for a long time.'
>
> *Bergen, May 1990 (in a BBC/OU televised interview).*

In the preceding chapters we have tried to incorporate positive suggestions alongside discussion of the issues, but the sheer scale of the problems often tends to dwarf the constructive things that are happening. It is easy to sound pessimistic when millions in Africa live their lives under the constant threat of famine, but our intention has always been to strike a positive note, certainly in conclusion if not throughout. Enough has already been achieved in global terms to ensure that a philosophical basis for progress and change that is realisable is in place: that is the achievement of the 'Brundtland process'. The pressure is on the politicians and the policy-makers to take up the challenge.

To underline the theme of local and global action we leave you with a summary of progress and action across the broad sweep of issues that we have been considering.

Progress towards 'a common future'

- Our attitudes and values are changing but they need to change further; for the first time it can be shown that the more developed world has vital interests in the solution of development problems in the less developed world, as well as environmental problems everywhere.

- The tropical rain forests must be seen as a 'sustainable resource' in terms of their 'total economic value', including both use and non-use value. This does not mean imposing westernised conservationist ideals or boycotting forest products. The way forward has been prescribed by the forest peoples of Endau Rompin in Malaysia: marketing sustainably produced forest products that take account of traditional patterns of trade and involve fully the indigenous peoples. *In July 1991, after much lobbying by groups like WWFN and Friends of the Earth, the World Bank agreed a policy to ban the funding of logging projects in the rain forest.*

- The food production problems of many African countries have been exacerbated by their incorporation into a global system of production and trade which seeks to expand production in ways that are neither sustainable nor equitable. However, farmers in drought-prone countries like Niger are showing that they can produce food in extremely difficult environments and are very responsive to the 'right kind of aid' – innovations linked to local participation which increase their income and protect the environment.

- Urban 'crisis' and poverty are inextricably linked in many cities of the less developed world. A World Bank policy paper (April 1991) calls for a new approach to urban policy, recommending widespread reforms related to infrastructure, management and financing, to make urban centres more productive, linking their economic performance with national development. One of the targets is easing congestion in cities like Bangkok and Mexico City. These are ambitious proposals in line with UNCED thinking, but they require major inputs of hard cash and the onus rests with the industrialised countries.

- Mineral extraction continues to have an extensive impact on landscapes around the world. Legislation can help to control the process, as shown in Canada and the UK, but the search for alternatives must have more effect in the longer term. This has a number of implications, particularly in terms of energy generation, but in other fields also. In the UK, for example, a shift of emphasis from road to rail transport (from private to public) would reduce the requirement for hard core aggregates needed in road building programmes. Such a policy shift would bring other benefits.

- Much progress has been made in the sphere of producing alternative energy sources, especially in the Scandanavian countries, notably Denmark. The technology exists to improve efficiency and reduce dependency on the fossil fuels. What is needed is greater political will allied to increasing co-operation from the world of industry and commerce. The richer nations can help the poorer nations in terms of improving the conditions for constructive aid and technology transfer.

- Ozone depletion and global warming pose significant threats for everyone on the planet. In both cases prevention has to be seen as the best remedy and the international community has made a serious start to secure agreements which will at least limit the speed at which things get worse. The policy changes needed are consistent with the changes needed to solve many other environmental problems, and this fact makes these issues a high priority on the global political agenda. It is down to individual nations to put their own houses in order, however, and in this respect countries like Norway are setting an important example for the rest of the world.

• International co-operation and agreement on global environmental issues is both practicable and feasible. The agreed 50 year moratorium on exploiting Antarctica reached in April 1991, after first the USA and Japan and then Germany and the UK had climbed down from their previous positions of intransigence, emphasises what can be achieved with a mixture of political will and sustained pressure from environmental groups internationally. In terms of achieving sustainable development there are many areas of policy where changes are happening and must continue to happen, nationally and internationally. Specifically, we cite:

> *Policy instruments*: nationally economic instruments are vital (the polluter pays, environmental taxation) linked to long-term infrastructural changes and education. This applies particularly to the richest nations.

> *Assessing development*: present ways of measuring economic development, like GNP and GDP must be changed to reflect environmental impact and the use of resources.

> *Internationalism*: policy links between the more developed and the less developed world must reflect more progressive approaches to the issues of debt, trade, the pricing of raw materials and commodities, and equity generally.

• Finally we return to values and the words of a respected man of letters, Raymond Williams:

'None of this is going to be easy. Deep changes of belief will be necessary, not just conveniently, where they are in fact impossible, among the power elites and the rich classes of the world, but in all of us who are now practically embedded in this general situation. We are bound to encounter the usual human reluctance to change, and we must accept that the changes will be very considerable and will have to be negotiated rather than imposed. [We must act] in a kind of good faith which is in fact rare.'

Socialism and Ecology, SERA, 1982.

Antarctica – the last wilderness?

BBC/OU Productions (1991) Programmes 1–8 in Environment Series (U206). Producer: Eleanor Morris.

Bernstein *et al.* (eds.) (1990) *The Food Question: Profits vs. People?* Earthscan.

J. Blunden (1991) 'Mineral resources' and 'The environmental impact of mining and minerals processing' in *Energy, Resources and Environment,* edited by J. Blunden and A. Reddish, Hodder and Stoughton.

I. Bowler (1991) 'Temperate agriculture' in *Environment, Population and Development,* edited by P. Sarre, Hodder and Stoughton.

S. Brown (1990) 'Humans and their environments: changing attitudes', in *Environment and Society*, edited by J. Silvertown and P. Sarre, Hodder and Stoughton.

C. Conroy and M. Litvinoff (1988) *The Greening of Aid-Sustainable Livelihoods in Practice,* Earthscan.

R. Franke and B. Chasin (1981) 'Peasants, peanuts, profits and pastoralists' in *Ecologist, 11*, No. 4, pp.156–168.

J. H. Gibbons *et al.* (1989) 'Strategies for energy use' in *Scientific American*, September 1989 (pp. 86–93).

A. G. Gilbert (1991) 'Urban problems in the Third World' in *Environment, Population and Development,* edited by P. Sarre, Hodder and Stoughton.

O. Greene (1991) 'Tackling global warming' in *Global Environmental Issues*, edited by P.M. Smith and K. Warr, Hodder and Stoughton.

J. Gribben and M. Kelly (1989) *Winds of Change: Living with the Greenhouse Effect,* Hodder and Stoughton.

D. Grigg (1991) 'World agriculture: productivity and sustainability' in *Environment, Population and Development*, edited by P. Sarre, Hodder and Stoughton.

J. Lovelock (1990) *The Ages of Gaia: A Biography of our Living Earth*, Bantam.

C. Miller and P. Garside (1991) 'The impact of manufacturing industry on the environment' in *Energy, Resources and Environment*, edited by J. Blunden and A. Reddish, Hodder and Stoughton.

R. Nash (1989) *The Rights of Nature: A History of Environmental Ethics*, University of Wisconsin Press.

D. Oliver, D. Elliott and A. Reddish (1991) 'Sustainable energy futures' in *Energy, Resources and Environment*, edited by J. Blunden and A. Reddish, Hodder and Stoughton.

The Open University (1974) *The Earth's Physical Resources* (S266), The Open University Press.

P. Pakkasen (1988) *Leading Issues in Thailand's Development Transformation 1960-1990,* Economic Research Institute, Bangkok.

D. Pearce *et al.* (1989) *Blueprint for a Green Economy*, Earthscan.

D. Pepper (1984) *The Roots of Modern Environmentalism*, Croom Helm.

D. Phantumvanit (1987) *Thailand: Natural Resources Profile*, Oxford University Press.

M. Redclift (1987) *Sustainable Development: Exploring the Contradictions*, Methuen and Co. Ltd.

A. Reddish (1991) 'Energy resources' in *Energy, Resources and Environment*, edited by J. Blunden and A. Reddish, Hodder and Stoughton.

S. Ross (1991) 'Atmospheres and climatic change' in *Global Environmental Problems*, edited by P.M. Smith and K. Warr, Hodder and Stoughton.

J. Seymour and H. Girardet (1987) *Blueprint for a Green Planet*, Dorling Kindersley.

J. Silvertown (1990) 'Earth as an environment for life', 'Inhabitants of the biosphere' and 'Ecosystems and populations' in *Environment and Society*, edited by J. Silvertown and P. Sarre, Hodder and Stoughton.

I. G. Simmons (1990) 'The impact of human societies on their environments' in *Environment and Society,* edited by J. Silvertown and P. Sarre, Hodder and Stoughton.

P. M. Smith (1991) 'Global development issues' in *Global Environmental Issues*, edited by P.M. Smith and K. Warr, Hodder and Stoughton.

P. M. Smith (1991) 'Sustainable development and equity' in *Global Environmental Issues*, edited by P.M. Smith and K. Warr, Hodder and Stoughton.

L. Starke (1990) *Signs of Hope*, Oxford University Press.

United Nations World Commission on Environment and Development (1987) *Our Common Future (The Brundtland Report)*, Oxford University Press.

UNCED (1990) *Bergen Conference Papers,* 8–16 May 1990.

K. Warr (1991) 'The Ozone Layer' in *Global Environmental Problems*, edited by P. M. Smith and K. Warr, Hodder and Stoughton.

P. Woodhouse (1991) 'Farming a wetland ecosystem: rice cultivation in Asia' in *Environment, Population and Development,* edited by P. Sarre, Hodder and Stoughton.

Index

Acknowledgements

Grateful acknowledgement is made to the following sources for permission to reproduce material in this book:

Text

Leggett, J. (1991), 'Face the facts George', *The Guardian,* 1 February 1991, Guardian Newspapers.

Figures

Figure 1.4: C.B. Cox and P.D. Moore (1980), *Biogeography,* 3rd edition, Blackwell Scientific Publications Ltd; Figure 3.3: J. Vidal (1990), 'New Gods in the jungle', *The Guardian,* 2 March 1990, Guardian Newspapers; Figure 6.1: J. Blunden (1985), *Mineral Resources and their Management,* Longman Group UK; Figures 7.1, 7.2, 7.3 and 7.4: *BP Statistical Review of World Energy* (1990), British Petroleum PLC; Figures 8.1 and 8.2: *SORG (UK Stratospheric Ozone Review Group),* 1988 Report. Reproduced by permission of the Controller of Her Majesty's Stationery Office; Figure 8.3: *SORG (UK Stratospheric Ozone Review Group),* 1990 Report. Reproduced by permission of the Controller of Her Majesty's Stationery Office; Figure 8.4: P.D. Jones and T.M.L. Wigley (1990), *Scientific American,* No 263 (2), pp 66-73. Information supplied by P.D. Jones, Climatic Research Unit, University of East Anglia; Figure 8.5: Charles Keeling / Carbon Dioxide Center. © John and Mary Gribbin 1990. Extracted from *Hothouse Earth,* published by Black Swan. All rights reserved; Figure 8.6: J. Houghton *et al.* (1990), *Climatic Change: The IPCC Scientific Assessment,* Cambridge University Press. © 1990 Intergovernmental Panel on Climate Change.

Photographs

Nigel Cattlin/Holt Studios Photograph Library: pp.1, 28, 67; National Trust Photographic Library/Joe Cornish: p.4; NASA/Science Photo Library: p.5; Jorge's Estudio/The Image Bank: p.9; K.T. Marsland, Department of Zoology, Oxford: p.14; Adrian Warren/ARDEA: p.15; Barry Lewis/Network: p.16; Mary Cherry/Holt Studios Photograph Library: p.18; Anthony J. Coulson: p.21; Peter Thornton/Lakeland Photographic: p.25; A.F. Kersting: p.27; Greenpeace/Miller: p.36 top; Greenpeace/Hodson: p.36 bottom; Mark Edwards/Still Pictures: pp.38, 41 right, 42, 48, 50, 54, 56, 61, 64, 84, 87, 88, 98, 117, 120 top and bottom, 122, 124, 127, 148, 154; Edward Parker/Still Pictures: pp.41 left, 53; Eleanor Morris/BBC: pp.20, 45, 46, 58 top and bottom, 59 (three), 94 top and bottom; David Beatty/Susan Griggs Agency: pp.52, 175; Mike England: p.72; Paul Smith/Open University: pp.74, 77 left and right, 80 bottom, 82, 150, 156, 159, 161 top and bottom, 162, 163; David Hoffman/Still Pictures: p.80 top; Rheinbraun Aktiengesellschaft: pp.92, 100; Douglas Dickens Photo Library: p.95; Mike Williams Photography: pp.102, 173; Stoke-on-Trent City Council: p.104 left and right; Martin Bond/Science Photo Library: p.110; Igor Kostin/Sygma: p.111; Earth Observation Satellite Co. (EOSAT), Lanham, Maryland, USA: p.114; John Mead/ Science Photo Library: p.125; C. Gilbert/British Antarctic Survey: p.128; NASA: p.131; Friends of the Earth: p.132; Greenpeace/Morgan: p.140 top and bottom; J. Allan Cash: pp.141, 166; Tomas Muscionico/Colorific!/Contact Press Images 1991: p.142; J.B. Diederich/Colorific!/Contact Press Images 1988: p.143; Greenpeace/Gowan: p.170; British Rail Inter City/Photograph courtesy of Barlow Reid: p.171; Cirroneau/AP Colour Library: p.176; D. Allan/British Antarctic Survey: p.183.